THE SAILOR, THE BARON AND THE DRESSMAKER

THE SAILOR, THE BARON AND THE DRESSMAKER

Glenn Martin

G.P. Martin Publishing

Published 2024 by G.P. Martin Publishing
Website: www.glennmartin.com.au
Contact: info@glennmartin.com.au

Book layout and cover design by the author
Typeset in Sitka 11 pt
Printed by Lulu.com
V070924

Cover design by the author.
Front cover: Siegfried Hottelmann (Baron von Einsiedel) and Ellen
Royall (see Figures 13 and 15)

ISBN: 978 0 6459543 3 3 (pbk.)

A catalogue record for this
book is available from the
NATIONAL LIBRARY OF AUSTRALIA
National Library of Australia

Contents

Table of Figures

1. Siegfried's place in my family and his own 1

2. Australia, the first time 4

3. Return to Germany.................................10

4. Exploring America, returning to Australia.................14

5. Approval to stay in Australia..........................20

6. September 1939: War is declared 27

7. Siegfried is interned.............................42

8. Tatura internment camps............................43

9. Siegfried at Tatura......................................48

10. Ellen joins Siegfried in internment....................50

11. Associates in the camp 55

12. Considering post-war life............................59

13. Release from internment............................64

14. Seigfried's involvement in organisations.................71

15. The end of internment 80

16. Life after release.................................81

17. Naturalisation 89

18. Reflections and afterthoughts...................93

Acknowledgments.................................... 100

The Author; Glenn Martin's books.................... 100

Notes 102

Sources for the images 113

Bibliography....................................... 118

Index..122

Table of Figures

Figure 1: The Dresden..2

Figure 2: The Gustav..3

Figure 3: Elephant handler feeding the elephants, Wirth's Circus, 1930s..5

Figure 4: The Magdeburg 8

Figure 5: The Adellen..10

Figure 6: Count von Einsiedel in America, 1930 12

Figure 7: The Tisnaren 14

Figure 8: Carn Brae at 32 Florence Street, Port Pirie.....................18

Figure 9: Advertisement for Wirth's Circus, 1930s 21

Figure 10: The Sydney Trocadero, 1930s 23

Figure 11: Boarding house at 134 Forest Road, Arncliffe............... 24

Figure 12: Poster for the movie, "Forty Thousand Horsemen"...... 28

Figure 13: Siegfried Hottelmann, photo from police file............... 29

Figure 14: The William Macarthur...31

Figure 15: Ellen Royall, from police file 35

Figure 16: Kenton Court in Cathedral Street, Woolloomooloo....... 38

Figure 17: Tatura Camp 1, 1943, showing division between compounds A and B 44

Figure 18: Tatura Camp 1..45

Figure 19: Tatura Camp 3; woodcuts of the camp, by Ludwig Hirschfeld-Mack.. 46

Figure 20: Knitted items for Tatura internees' enterprise.............52

Figure 21: Johannes Frerck..56

Figure 22: Hottelmann family photo with Dannenbergs 60

Figure 23: Sketch of Tatura Camp 3 by C. Gluckner 62

Figure 24: Justice William Simpson 65

Figure 25: Map of Germany 67

Figure 26: Australian Sea Scouts in 1930s 72

Figure 27: Hitler marching with S.S. officers 74

Figure 28: Wolf Klaphake 77

Figure 29: Siegfried, Ellen and two children, 1945 80

Figure 30: The Canberra 81

Figure 31: Newspaper headlines in 1946 82

Figure 32: The house in Bestic Street, Rockdale 84

Figure 33A: Marriage certificate, 1939 85

Figure 33B: Amendment to marriage certificate, 1948 86

Figure 34: The Westralia 87

Figure 35: Passenger Arrival card for Siegfried Hottelmann 91

Figure 36: Holzminden in West Germany, 1983 92

Figure 37: Family tree with Glenn Martin and Ellen Royall 96

Figure 38: Carrs Park in the 1920s 97

Figure 39. Plaque of Siegfried made in Tatura internment camp .. 99

People face a situation from either need or opportunity (potential). But, the third option is, they can face it with **aristocratic nonchalance**.

Dina Nayeri, author of *Who Gets Believed?*

1. Siegfried's place in my family and his own

Among the direct ancestors in my family tree there were three convicts: unwilling migrants. All of the others were intentional migrants who planned their migration to this country openly, as a break from their traditional community in order to embark on a new life. Among my other relatives there is just one who may have been opportunistic. Or, he knew what he intended to do, and planned his migration, but he did it in secret.

He was a German: Siegfried Hottelmann. He came to Australia in 1938, and deserted the ship on which he was a sailor. The atmosphere in Germany had become stridently nationalistic, with Hitler on the rise, and it was already clear to many that a war was looming in Europe. Siegfried was of soldier-age: twenty-seven, having been born in 1911.

What was Siegfried's attitude towards Germany and towards the prospect of war? It helps (although it complicates things) to know that he belonged to an ancient family. His mother's name was von Einsiedel. She was a baroness, and the von Einsiedel name is renowned in German history. Johann August von Einsiedel, 1754-1837, was a rationalist philosopher and a friend of the philosopher Goethe. Johann was convinced that a golden age was imminent, when wars would cease, and when inequality, injustice, and selfishness would disappear.[1]

There is an Einsiedel Dam in Saxony. It supplies drinking water to the city of Chemnitz. It was finished in 1894, and is the third oldest in Germany.

Another member of the von Einsiedel family, however, was Count Heinrich von Einsiedel, who became a fighter pilot in the German Luftwaffe. He was shot down near Stalingrad in 1942, and quickly became aligned with the Russians. He joined the Free German National Committee in Moscow, and leaflets with his name on them were aerially broadcast to German soldiers. He was a great grandson of the first German Chancellor, Otto von Bismarck. The leaflets said, "The war against Russia is stupid and without a chance. This my great grandfather said time and time again".[2]

After the war, Heinrich von Einsiedel was convicted by a United States military court of spying for the Russians.[3] I have not been able to establish his precise link to Siegfried's mother's family, but there are only limited possibilities.

Siegfried Hottelmann told an inquiry in 1946 that the von Einsiedel name went back to before 1350, as did the title of Baron. He was the heir to that title. His father was Max Hottelmann, a prominent German engineer, who had constructed what was then the largest dam in Europe, opened in 1911.[4] Siegfried was born at Holzminden, Lower Saxony.[5] His father was killed during the First World War, and his mother died two years later. Siegfried explained to the inquiry that he was sent to live with his grandfather, but found him "too severe to live with".[6]

The Australian government did not automatically release German internees at the end of the Second World War. It held an inquiry to assess who should be deported and who should be allowed to remain in Australia. It was conducted by Justice William Simpson.[7]

After the death of his parents, Siegfried was sent to school in Hamburg, to be educated for the role of Baron von Einsiedel. He said, "I read books about adventure and decided I would go to sea".[8] He felt it necessary to not use the name "von Einsiedel", and managed to obtain a passport in the name "Hottelmann", his father's name. He first went to sea in December 1927, aged 16, on the ship *Dresden*. He appears in the passenger list.[9]

Figure 1: The Dresden, 1927, bound for New York

The ship, a steam ship with two funnels, was originally called the *Zeppelin*. It was built in 1915, but was laid up for the duration of World War I, and then renamed the *Ormuz* and used on routes between Germany, America and Australia. It was handed over to Britain as part of war reparations in 1920, but was sold back to its German owners in 1927 and renamed the *Dresden*. Its maiden voyage was from Bremen to New York. Siegfried sailed as far as Queenstown (in Cork, Ireland; now called Cobh). (The ship was lost seven years later when it hit a rock off the coast of Norway. It partially sank and it was unable to be saved.)[10]

Siegfried did not go home to Germany. He boarded another ship, the *Gustav*, this time as a sailor, an Able Seaman and Rigger.[11] The *Gustav* was a German sailing ship, a four-masted barque with a steel hull. It had left Vifstarval (in Sweden) on 30 September 1927 for Melbourne carrying timber and wood pulp.

Figure 2: The Gustav

However, in the North Sea and the English Channel it was buffeted by a huge gale. Waves swept over the barque and a portion of the bulwarks was washed away. Minor leaks developed in the holds, and the master decided to make for Ireland. While the ship was on land for the repairs, trouble developed among the crew, who disliked the prospect of an even rougher trip ahead, and the master dismissed them and engaged new men. Siegfried was among those engaged.[12]

2. Australia, the first time

The *Gustav* put to sea from Queenstown on Christmas Eve, 1927. "Good progress was made until it rounded the Cape of Good Hope. She then ran into a number of icefloes and drifting bergs at intervals of between 200 and 300 miles. The master and crew spent an anxious time while sailing in that region. A keen watch had to be kept for the large bergs, but the voyage was completed in safety." The voyage took 92 days from Ireland to Melbourne, arriving on 26 March 1928.[1]

After unloading its cargo, the ship was to load wheat at Geelong and transport it to the United Kingdom.[2] However, again, trouble with the crew occurred. A report in *The Argus* (Melbourne) on 14 April 1928 stated, "Nine of the crew of the *Gustav* deserted from the ship yesterday. Apparently the deserters, with the prospect of another long voyage, decided to tempt fortune in Australia. One is a Dutchman and the remaining eight are Germans. According to a clause in the laws governing the landing of aliens (ie non-British citizens), the master of the *Gustav* was liable to a fine of £100 for each member of the crew who may attempt to remain in Australia without the necessary passport and papers."[3]

Siegfried was one of the deserters. He admitted this to the internment inquiry in 1946.[4] This was his first trip to Australia. He returned a decade later, deserted ship again, met and married a relative on my father's side of the family after a quick romance, and after the Second World War began, he was interned for the duration of the war. He was sent to Tatura Camp in Victoria, and his Australian wife joined him.

As a seventeen-year-old deserting ship in Australia in 1928, Siegfried seemed to be in search of adventure, as well as wanting to leave his home and family in Germany behind him. Perhaps his longing for adventure was not unusual. Schutt, the master of the *Gustav*, was unperturbed about the desertions from his ship. He said he had received "more applications for the positions than he had vacancies to fill. Most of the applications were from young Australians anxious to experience life under sail".[5] This was at a time when sail was being rapidly superseded by steam.

Siegfried found himself a job on a farm at Alexandra, Victoria. It is a rural town 130 kilometres north-east of Melbourne. Later, probably at the end of May 1928, he took a position as a seaman on the *Milora*, a steamer which traded around the coastal ports of Australia. (It was owned by Australasian United Steam Navigation Co.; it was condemned in 1935 and sunk off Port Phillip Bay.[6]) He remained on that ship for several months, until an accident occurred and he was hurt. He left the ship in Brisbane in November 1928. He found his way back to Melbourne and took odd jobs, then he worked for about six months as a boundary rider on a farm at Hopetoun in northwest Victoria, around 400 kilometres from Melbourne.[7]

He told the inquiry that when he was on this sojourn in Australia he joined Wirth's Circus and toured New Zealand for six months as an elephant driver. The judge at the internment inquiry asked him, "What do you know about elephants?" and Siegfried answered, "I do not know anything, but I wanted to see the world and I was prepared to work my way."[8]

Figure 3: Elephant handler feeding the elephants, Wirth's Circus, 1930s

It is somewhat vague as to when and where Siegfried joined the circus. He refers to stowing away on a ship to return to Australia, and we have to assume that he stowed away to go to New Zealand and joined the circus once there. It might be that he needed to stow away because he had already deserted a ship and he may have been on notice with the customs authorities.

Wirth's Circus, which billed itself as "The Greatest Show on Earth", toured New Zealand many times, beginning in 1889, and it tended to go there every two years or so.[9] The circus had a performance schedule that was almost non-stop, touring towns right around Australia and New Zealand, even small towns.[10] It might stay in a large city like Sydney, Melbourne or Auckland for two weeks or more, but in many places it stayed for one night only, packing up everything in the morning and moving on again. Wirth's had about 120 people in the company, in addition to its many animals, big and small. It usually travelled by its own special train. It toured New Zealand for about four months, starting in late November 1929, with its last performance being at Auckland on 20 March 1930.

Curiously, Wirth's Circus was started by a German family, who emigrated to Australia in 1856. In 1930 it was still run by the same Wirth family. Perhaps they were sympathetic to a young, enthusiastic German lad who arrived wanting adventure. Wirth's had become Australia's pre-eminent circus. In its early days it travelled using bullock wagons and steamers, and when the railways were established, they had their own special trains. In its heyday, the circus had a large menagerie of elephants, lions and tigers, horses, bears and baboons.[11]

Siegfried told the inquiry that he came back to Australia on a Norwegian ship. There were rules in both countries about "aliens" entering the country, and Siegfried was already a deserter from the *Gustav*, so it would make sense if he was a stowaway in crossing the Tasman.

In New Zealand, the circus started at Invercargill on the south island and worked its way northwards towards Auckland. It was the fiftieth year of the circus, its jubilee, and George Wirth, one of the owners, had been in the US buying new acts for the New Zealand tour.[12] After Invercargill the circus performed at Ellesmere, Ashburton, Timaru, Christchurch, Lyttelton, Wellington, Hawkes Bay, the Bay of Plenty, Palmerston, Foxton, Hawera and numerous

6

other towns, before it finished up at Auckland.[13] The circus used the ship *Katoa* to travel between the north and south islands, then a train for the journey between towns.

One wonders how Siegfried managed with the elephants. When the elephants wanted to play, they played. In January 1929 a New Zealand newspaper reported on an incident in Melbourne: "There was considerable excitement in the city when six elephants attached to Wirth's Circus, just landed from a steamer, bolted through the streets. No damage was done but traffic was disorganised."[14]

The circus had nine elephants. Princess, the eldest, said to be 123 years of age, weighed four and a half tons, and ate nine bales of straw for one meal.[15] Some of the elephants did not perform in the circus; their job was to assist in the loading and unloading of the trucks, "shunting" them along the tracks. At one of the towns there was an incident when an elephant in a railway van rocked the van so violently that it jumped the rails, bringing the train to a sudden halt. It took four hours to get the van back on the tracks.[16,17]

Once, when the circus was in Sydney, Jess, one of the elephants, escaped from Erskineville Park and went cavorting around the town. It was a moonlit night, and a man looked out of his window at 2:30 a.m. and saw her dancing on the lawn – she was one of the dancing elephants. She trumpeted loudly, waking many local residents, then she stomped into a yard and began to pull trees out of the ground with her trunk, tossing them away. A circus attendant came to collect her, but Jess chased him away and trampled a fence down. "When more men from the circus arrived, Jess was trying her strength on a two-foot-thick elm, but they finally persuaded her to go home." The elephant's keeper said she got away by breaking her chain. Wirth's Circus repaired the damage to property. This was reported in a New Zealand newspaper.[18]

Another time, one of the attendants was mauled. He was fastening an elephant with a stake when she became annoyed. She seized him with her trunk, lifted him from the ground, and began to squeeze him. He was bent over backwards and in so much pain that he nearly lost consciousness. Then the elephant put him down on the ground and jostled him with her head. The attendant was taken to hospital, but he was alright, and he was allowed to leave.[19]

It was not unusual for the elephants to get away from the circus and go exploring. When this happened at Macksville, on the New South Wales north coast, the elephant was found the next morning on a dairy farm, among the cows.[20] The occupation of elephant attendant was not without its challenges and hazards. But no experience was required, just a conviction that you could do it.

When the circus came back to Sydney after its New Zealand tour, it was on board the *Ulimaroa*. The elephants travelled on-deck, with one leg secured by a stout chain. The circus people travelled on the ship too, performers and crew alike.[21] One assumes that when the ship left, Siegfried was waiting for a ship to stow away on.

Was there a risk in stowing away on a ship? Yes, at both ends of the journey. In July 1930, a Yugoslavian man was arrested in Sydney off the *Ulimaroa*. He had stowed away on the ship to New Zealand and had been caught and refused entry to New Zealand.[22] In another incident, five stowaways were discovered in the *Ulimaroa* at Wellington in the customary search as it readied to sail to Sydney. The men were sent ashore, but just before sailing time, two of them regained the ship. They were found, and were again removed from the vessel.[23]

Figure 4: The Magdeburg

As a now-experienced seaman, Siegfried found himself a job on the crew of a ship going back to Europe. He told the internment inquiry that he returned to Germany in 1930 on the steam ship

Magdeburg. This ship was owned by the German Australian Line. It was 6,128 tons, and it carried cargo between Australia and Europe. It had been to Australia three times previously, making the trip between Europe and Australia in six to ten weeks.[24]

The *Magdeburg* arrived in Adelaide on 19 May 1930, and was contracted to carry wool to a number of German and Belgian ports. With its cargo of 10,000 bales loaded, it left Sydney on 25 June. It arrived at Antwerp, Belgium on 6 August, a much faster trip than Siegfried's three-month voyage to Australia on the *Gustav*. At Antwerp, Siegfried was about 400 kilometres from Holzminden by road, or he may have gone by train, via Brussels and Cologne.

3. Return to Germany

I think Siegfried was disappointed when he returned home. In an interview with the police at Darlinghurst on 6 September 1939 (war had been declared on 3 September 1939 and the police were monitoring the presence of Germans in the community), Siegfried said he returned to Germany and remained there for two months. I think Siegfried's return home merely confirmed that his outlook on life diverged markedly from that of his relatives, and he left again, looking for another job on a ship.

Siegfried told the internment inquiry that he worked as a sailor for about two months on the *Adellen*, a British ship.[1] The *Adellen* was new, launched in September 1930 in Glasgow for a London company. It was 7,984 tons, a steel-hulled motor vessel.[2] It carried cargo between Britain and America. It was fast: on one trip, it passed west at Lloyd's Signal Station on the south coast of Cornwall on 1 May, on its way to America, and was back at Hull, England on 4 July.[3] Accordingly, Siegfried's two-month stint probably consisted of one voyage to America and back.

The *Adellen* landed at Amsterdam on 21 March 1931, and it then travelled back to America. This is most likely the voyage that Siegfried went on. The *Adellen* continued in service until 22 February 1942, when it was torpedoed by a German U-boat south of Greenland and it sank, losing thirty-six of its forty-eight crew.[4]

Figure 5: The Adellen

Siegfried went to Hamburg, and he said that from mid-1931 until 1934 he worked as an interpreter.[5] However, Siegfried could be selective about what he disclosed and to whom he disclosed it. One of his daughters said that her father had told her that he went to Rostock, on the northern coast of Germany, at the head of the Warnow River (about 190 kilometres from Hamburg), and completed an Economics degree at Rostock University (an ancient institution, founded in 1419). Following this, he ran an insurance company. He also travelled to Russia; there were members of the von Einsiedel family there, with diplomatic connections.[6] (This may make sense of Heinrich von Einsiedel's prompt liaison with the Russians in 1942.)

There is an abbreviated account of Siegfried's activities from when he submitted an objection to his internment, in December 1940. He states that he had been a salesman in Hamburg. We could call this a loose substantiation that he was in business there.[7]

We know that he went to sea again, serving on British ships and those of other nations. When he arrived in Australia in 1938, Siegfried was holding a passport issued at Hamburg on 7 September 1935. In 1936 he left Germany permanently.[8] He went to America as a seaman on the ship *Hagen*, arriving at Boston, Massachusetts on 3 September 1936.[9]

His activities in America are described only scantily, and they were not discussed at the internment inquiry. But there were reasons he might have been interested in America. In 1930 there was another member of the von Einsiedel family in the country, a count. He appears in a curious newspaper article, which was copied without alteration by several other US newspapers.

The text of the article says: "Although he is heir to an estate near Essen, Germany and calls a castle there 'home', young Count Von Einsiedel works as a laborer in Henry Ford's automobile plant in Detroit and punches a time clock. The young count (inset) who is 20, plans to work a year in the factory before returning to Germany. He believes he may turn his ancestral home (pictured above) into an automobile factory".[10]

Despite the humble situation described – a labourer in an automobile factory – the news article is a designed piece like a postcard, consisting of a photograph of the Count's impressive castle in Essen, Germany, set in a frame with the text below, and at the top of the photograph is a circular inset with the head of the Count. It is incongruous for a factory worker. The item must have been supplied to the newspaper by the family as a form of public relations.

Figure 6: Count von Einsiedel in America, 1930

COUNT PUNCHES CLOCK FOR FORD

Although he is heir to an 8,000-acre estate near Essen, Germany, and calls a castle there "home," young Count Von Einseidel works as a laborer in Henry Ford's automobile plant in Detroit and punches a time clock. The young count, inset, who is 20, plans to work a year in the factory before returning to Germany. He believes he may turn his ancestral home, above, into an automobile factory.

Siegfried no doubt knew about the count. (In the German structure of nobility, barons are above counts.) Siegfried and the count were close in age; the count may have been a cousin. We don't know much about Siegfried's family apart from the fact that his father was Maximilian Hottelmann, his mother was Ilse von

Einsiedel, and he had a grandfather who was alive when Siegfried left Germany.

Siegfried may have heard that the count had gone to America, and probably even knew why. So, perhaps Siegfried was interested in seeing what America had to offer. Moreover, Siegfried's daughter said that he went to Brazil where his aunt (his mother's sister) and his sister had settled. (This is the only indication we have that Siegfried had any sisters. Given the hereditary situation, it is quite clear that he had no brothers.)

The most likely time that he went to Brazil was soon after he arrived in America. However, we may note that in his application objecting to his internment, he does not mention it. In the question asking about what countries he had been to since leaving Germany, he mentions only the U.S.A.

Siegfried said on numerous occasions that his views were different from those of his family. The count was interested in establishing a car factory in Essen (200 kilometres east of Holzminden). In an interview with a newspaper after the end of the war, Siegfried said, "The (Einsiedel) estate has always been closely cultivated, and only home industries practised there. Our family pledge was to live off the land. It was just 'not done' for the German nobility to set up industries on their estates."[11]

This is no doubt a barb with the count in mind. Note, there is also irony in the fact that the 1946 newspaper headline was "Baron works as A.B. on steamer *Canberra*", using the same adulation for those bearing titles as the newspaper articles about the count in the US newspapers in 1930.

4. Exploring America, returning to Australia

So, apart from the report from his daughter, the only indication of how Siegfried spent his two years in America is given by the application he submitted in December 1940. We do know that he had a strong spirit of adventure and was willing to put his hand to anything. The application says that he worked as a sailor and a salesman. What he sold we don't know. It also says that he lived in California, at San Jose, Monterey, Los Angeles and San Francisco – all cities on the west coast.[1]

We know by the logic of time that Siegfried was in San Francisco in late July 1938, where he joined the *M.S. Tisnaren*, a Swedish merchant ship of 5,747 tons carrying cargo around the world. It had just come from Vancouver with a load of timber for Australia.[2] San Francisco was its last stop before Australia.[3] When Siegfried deserted ship in Adelaide in September 1938, the captain of the ship stated that he had been a crew member for one and a half months.[4]

Figure 7: The Tisnaren

Why did Siegfried choose to come to Australia? In 1946, when he was interviewed by a journalist, he said Australia to him was like the Land of the Sphinx for others – "Once you have been there, you always want to return".[5]

The *Tisnaren* arrived in Sydney on 25 August 1938, but was only there for a day. It sailed on to Melbourne and it was there for several days while the timber was unloaded.[6] The next port for the *Tisnaren* was Adelaide. It arrived on Friday 9 September.[7] The Adelaide Agricultural Show was opening, and the Swedish Ambassador was visiting for the show. However, there was no accommodation left in town, and the ambassador ended up staying on board the *Tisnaren*.[8] It was not a hardship: the ship only carried about twenty passengers each voyage, and the cabins on the ship were advertised as luxurious.[9]

The *Tisnaren* left again on Wednesday 14 September, bound for Queensland to pick up 8,700 tons of sugar to transport to London.[10] When the ship left Adelaide, Siegfried was not on it; he had deserted. Captain Samuelson notified Customs as he was obliged to do, as Siegfried was a Prohibited Immigrant, a German.[11] The police were notified.[12]

At the internment inquiry in 1946, Siegfried explained how he had been exposed in Adelaide as the heir to the von Einsiedel title. He said he visited a German ship in the port, and it so happened that an electrician on the ship recognised him. The man was the son of Siegfried's grandfather's gardener on the family estate in Lower Saxony.[13] Justice Simpson asked Siegfried, "Don't you want to be known as Baron von Einsiedel?" Siegfried replied, "I had different ideas from them, and I wanted to go to Australia again."

It may be that Siegfried visited the ship simply because it was German and he wanted to talk with fellow countrymen. However, this was a sensitive time. Increasingly there was the notion that war was looming. German merchant ships were still plying their trade, transporting goods around the world, and in September 1938, several were in Australian waters. The *Stassfurt*, the ship that Siegfried visited in Adelaide, was there to load 2,500 tons of lead for Germany. However, just two weeks later, a decision was made by all German merchant shipping companies to order all their ships on the high seas to return home immediately.[14] No explanation was given in the newspapers for this directive, but it was ominous. One reading of this action is that the shipping companies were seeking to protect their ships in the event of a war. Note that the ship on which Siegfried first went to sea, the *Dresden*, had been built in 1915 but was kept in dry dock for the entire First World War.

Siegfried told the inquiry that there were refugees on the *Stassfurt*. Justice Simpson did not ask where the refugees were from; clearly it was obvious to all present. But the way Siegfried discloses the information, it is also clear that he had not expected their presence. The refugees were Jews from Germany, seven of them. Their arrival in Australia was reported in the *Recorder* (Adelaide) on 16 September 1938 with the headline: "Can See People Smiling Again: Jewish Immigrant Is Happy".[15]

The person the journalist interviewed begged the journalist not to publish his name: "Please do not use my name. It is better to remain in the shadows. Promise not to use my name." With that assurance, the refugee told the journalist, "I have left a country where no one is laughing." But he was pleased with his first view of Australia. "Everyone to whom I have spoken has been polite. Perhaps it has been a Customs man or some other visitor to the ship. No German would do that now, since the Germans think that they are better men than us."

"Jews are not allowed to make money in Germany any more," he said. He knew it would be different in Australia, because everyone was so nice to him.

Strangely, Siegfried was just as worried as the Jewish refugee about being exposed. He told the inquiry, "Doubtless they went straight to the police and told them about me." It is not clear who "they" were. It may have been that Siegfried had already deserted his ship, so was concerned about being arrested as a German deserter. But it seemed that his fear related more to being recognised as a von Einsiedel.

This raises the question that, if Siegfried had just deserted ship, why would he visit another ship, and particularly a German ship? And was the refugee thinking of Siegfried when he spoke of "some other visitor to the ship" being polite to him? Perhaps Siegfried was wanting to get a sense of what things were currently like in Germany, given that he had been absent from there since 1936. He may have wanted personal confirmation that his decision to desert ship in Australia had been the right one. One imagines that he got it.

The captain of the *Tisnaren*, Knut Berner Samuelson, notified Customs and delivered Siegfried's passport to them.[16] The police were informed to be on the lookout for him.

According to the form that Captain Samuelson completed, Siegfried deserted on or about Sunday 11 September. Samuelson stated in a written note at the bottom of the form that he was of "good character as far as I am concerned."

The Collector of Customs, South Australia, notified the Secretary, Department of the Interior, Canberra, of the desertion, and that "A reward of £5 is offered by an Indemnity Company (Messrs. Gibbs Bright & Co.) for the recovery of this man who is regular seafaring by occupation". The indemnity company played a role because the ship was held responsible by Customs for the desertion of sailors, with a penalty of £100.[17]

Siegfried was not arrested. The South Australian Police Gazette posted a notice on 21 September 1938 to say that if Siegfried Emil Hottelmann was located, the Port Adelaide police should be advised. He had "deserted from the M.V. *Tisnaren*. Description: Native of Germany, seaman, born 1911, 5ft. 9in. high, fair complexion, dark-brown hair, blue eyes, oval face, speaks English".[18]

Desertion generally led to arrest, gaol and deportation. A Swedish sailor had deserted off the *Tisnaren* in 1935 in Fremantle and this was the outcome. The ship had left Fremantle on the Friday night, and the sailor was arrested the following Tuesday. The initial charge was vagrancy. The sailor failed a dictation test administered by the police (the government's way of preventing people from entering Australia by giving a test of fifty words in any language the authority chose).

In court, the sailor said that he had had several drinks at a hotel in Fremantle then gone to sleep. When he woke up, he went to the wharf and found his ship had gone. The matter was referred to the Minister for the Interior, who ordered deportation after the sailor had served three months' imprisonment.[19]

It is not known what Siegfried did for the next two months, but on 16 November 1938 he obtained work at Port Pirie as a winchman on a dredge which was operated by the South Australian Harbour Board.[20] On 17 December 1938 he signed onto the steamer *Mungana*, going to Sydney and arriving on 28 December. However, the ship was then laid up at Lime Street wharves and the crew were paid off.[21]

Siegfried took a train via Melbourne to return to Adelaide. On 30 December he visited the Immigration & Passports Office in Melbourne to let them know he was on his way back to Adelaide. Thus we learn that he must have put in an application to be allowed to stay in Australia when he was in Melbourne back in early September, before he even arrived at Adelaide. Mr F.J.R. Penhallhuriack, the Immigration and Passports Officer in Melbourne, refers in his memo back to 2 September and says Siegfried "would be glad to receive early advice as to whether he may remain in Australia". Siegfried showed the officer his rail ticket to get back to Adelaide, where he still had £12 in wages owing to him from his work on the dredge.[22]

The language is very polite and respectful. One imagines that Siegfried likewise treated the officials with appropriate deference, and was accustomed to being successful in his purposes. After his return to Adelaide in late December 1938, Siegfried waited to find out if he would be approved to stay in Australia. He collected his wages from his work on the dredge, and stayed at 32 Florence Street, Port Pirie.

Figure 8: Carn Brae at 32 Florence Street, Port Pirie

The place where Siegfried was staying was not a shabby sailors' bolt-hole; it was a stately home called Carn Brae (after a place in Redruth, Cornwall), built in 1909 for a Cornish engineer, Edward Moyle, who operated the adjacent cordial factory and public baths. It is made of local stone and features ornate ironwork. Significantly, perhaps, to Siegfried, it also featured stained glass windows that had been imported from Germany. It currently (in 2024) serves as a museum and also as luxury accommodation.[23]

In January 1939 he obtained further work as a sailor, this time on the *Aeon*, a coastal steamer. He was originally employed for six weeks. The steamer had a regular route between Adelaide, Sydney and Port Kembla. It loaded lead at Port Pirie for Sydney, and on the return trip it stopped at Port Kembla and loaded coal and coke for Adelaide.

The *Aeon* left Adelaide on 27 January 1939 with lead (and Siegfried). It arrived in Sydney on 2 February, and remained in dock unloading until 7 February. It left at midnight for Port Kembla, then stopped at Melbourne and was back at Port Pirie on 16 February with 3,197 tons of coke and 1,693 tons of small coal.[24]

The *Aeon*'s next trip from Port Pirie began on 23 February. This time it had 4,291 tons of lead and 500 tons of copper matte (manufactured from copper ore, an alloy consisting of copper and sulphur that is used in making many products, including cement, fertiliser and glass). It arrived in Sydney at six a.m. on 2 March, unloaded and left again on 8 March, having left at 1:21 a.m. for Port Kembla. It picked up 2,700 tons of coke and 1,700 tons of coal. It was back in Adelaide on 16 March and was expected to be in port for a few days.[25]

5. Approval to stay in Australia

Siegfried must have collected his pay as soon as he arrived in port and gone straight back to his accommodation at 32 Florence Street to see if any letters had arrived for him. The letter notifying him that he had been approved to stay in Australia permanently would have been there; it was sent on 1 March, signed by F. Terry, the Collector of Customs for South Australia. The only requirement on his part was to pay the £1 landing permit. A memo from the Sub-Collector of Customs at Port Pirie to the Collector of Customs at Port Adelaide shows that the fee was paid on 17 March.[1]

On 29 March, Siegfried was informed that his passport was in the Office of the Sub-Collector of Customs, Port Pirie, for collection.[2]

There is one aspect of the approval that is curious: in the late 1930s, the Department of the Interior required refugee immigrants to have personal funds of at least £200, and there is no mention of this requirement in Siegfried's correspondence (likewise, there is no suggestion he is a refugee). Australia was accepting Jewish people from Germany, but they had to satisfy this requirement.

By February 1939, "few refugees now are receiving landing permits unless they have at least £500.... the Secretary of the Department of the Interior (Mr Carrodus) emphasised that the Government was hand-picking refugee migrants and was determined that the 15,000 to be allowed entry in the next three years would be of the most suitable types. For months past the Aliens Branch of the Department has been flooded with applications, which now total more than 40,000. and there is a wide range for selection. Unless a male refugee applicant is a skilled worker, particularly in a branch of industry in which there is a shortage, he has little hope of getting a permit if he possesses only the minimum landing money".[3]

The same news article adds: "Most of the refugee migrants are embarking from London or from Southern European ports. None are coming direct from Germany." Siegfried is indeed an unusual case. It may be noted that the refugees on the *Stassfurt* were also an unusual case, having come directly from Germany.

Siegfried still needed to get his passport back. On 29 March, the Collector of Customs wrote to Siegfried to inform him that German Passport 16160 issued in his favour at Hamburg on 7th of

September 1935 was waiting for him to collect at the office of the Sub-Collector of Customs, Port Pirie. We don't know when Siegfried picked up his passport, but an administrative follow-up within the Customs office on 27 June confirms that the passport had indeed been collected.[4]

Given the promptness with which Siegfried acted on his approval to stay in Australia, it is most likely that he collected his passport just as promptly. Siegfried continued working on the *Aeon* until 24 May, when he finished up in Sydney. That date is confirmed by Captain Turner of Howard Smith when he was interviewed by the police in July 1939.

Each time the *Aeon* arrived in Sydney it spent a few days unloading its cargo, so Siegfried would have had a few days of leisure. Up to this point he had only been in Sydney for a few days: one day, 25 August 1938, on the *Tisnaren*, and the period over Christmas in 1938 when the *Mungana* was laid up at Lime Street wharf. The *Aeon* was in Sydney from 2 to 7 February, from 2 to 8 March, ad arrived again on 31 March and 21 April. We can guess that Siegfried had seen enough of Sydney to want to see more, and perhaps even want to stay there.

Figure 9: Advertisement for Wirth's Circus, 1930s

Moreover, there was something happening in Sydney in which Siegfried would have been very interested: Wirth's Circus. It had arrived in Sydney in early April 1939, with its opening performance on 1 April. It continued with performances right through the Easter period and up to 30 April. [5] Given his experiences with the circus in 1929, one imagines that he was excited by its being in Sydney just as he arrived. Wirth's Circus was, in any case, an exciting event; this circus was "The Greatest Show on Earth".

Siegfried had secured accommodation in Sydney at 8 Springfield Avenue, Potts Point (Kings Cross).

It was a street that consisted mostly of buildings three to five stories high that could be described as comfortable lodgings. It was about ten minutes' walk from Woolloomooloo.

The circus was camped at the corner of Oxford and Riley Streets at Darlinghurst, just a few minutes' walk from Springfield Avenue.[6] One imagines Siegfried looking forward to seeing the elephants and all the other animals again, refreshing the memories of his youthful adventure in New Zealand, and seeing the huge tent and all the performers and workers, not to mention the crowds and the excited children.

Siegfried Hottelmann and Ellen Royall could have met in a multitude of places, perhaps not even in Sydney, but thousands of people came to see the circus in Sydney, and it is easy to imagine that Ellen did too. It was unusual for the circus to stay so long in one place – normally it would stay in a big city for a week or two, but this time it was a full month.

Ellen would have come from the boarding house where she lived in Arncliffe, not too far – about ten kilometres, getting the bus to Rockdale Station, then the train into the city. She may have come with friends, or with siblings, of whom there were several. And Siegfried had periods in Sydney while he was waiting for the ship to unload and load.

Yet, whether they went to the circus or not, there is information from Siegfried's daughter that the place where they met was the Trocadero, at a dinner-dance. The Trocadero was a large dance and concert hall in George Street, near Town Hall Station. It was built in art deco style in 1936, and stayed open until 1971 (when it was replaced by a cinema). It was hugely popular with young people. My mother was sixteen in 1939, and she went there many times with friends. It was exciting and glamorous. There was a resident "big band" called the Trocadero Orchestra and the hall could accommodate up to two thousand people for dances and balls.[7]

Figure 10: The Sydney Trocadero, 1930s

Advertisements for the Trocadero in April and May 1939 say the Trocadero is an "Ideal Rendezvous for Pre-wedding and all other Social Gatherings!" There is a dance every Saturday afternoon, with a special dance enclosure. You can listen to the Trocadero Swing Concert Orchestra. On Friday nights there is a "Cabaret at 9, with novelties, balloons, floor show and supper".[8]

Siegfried and Ellen meet, at the Trocadero, and romance flares between them. They resolve to get married. Why? What is the rush? War is often the catalyst for people to get married, particularly if the man is in the army or expected to be in the army soon. Marriage is an offer of hope to the man in such a situation, and a hope for both of them for the future.

But the impetus here is not the same. For Siegfried, the perceived impetus is that he would strengthen his hold on Australia through Ellen. Although, the law did not work that way. In fact, once an Australian (Ellen) married a German (Siegfried), the Australian wife became German by marriage.[9] This would probably have been known to Ellen, and perhaps to Siegfried as well. In any case, Siegfried had already been given permanent residency in Australia.

It may well be that the reason Siegfried and Ellen got married was because they were in love with each other. It was an appropriate time in life for both of them to get married. They were adults in their twenties, and times were uncertain. He was personable and urbane. He was impetuous, but seemingly able to manage the adventures he took on. He had travelled around the world and explored foreign countries, looking after himself and making easy connections with other people. He had made the decision not to return to his home country and his ancestral family, and evidently he was ready, all of a sudden, to establish a new life with someone in Australia.

Ellen was independent of her parents, living in a boarding house at Arncliffe run by Mrs Gertrude Buckley, and working as a dressmaker for a firm in the city. She was likewise sociable, and it seems that she was lovely. She had friends and siblings who were getting married around this time. Perhaps the fact that he was foreign was an attraction. Perhaps the failure of her parents' marriage fuelled in her an urge to have a successful marriage of her own. Ellen had been young (five years old) when her parents divorced, and she was twelve when her father remarried.[10]

Figure 11: Boarding house at 134 Forest Road, Arncliffe

On 1 July 1939, Siegfried and Ellen Royall were married.[11] Ellen's mother was Blanche Royall (born Eaglestone). Blanche's sister was Elizabeth Hannah (Eaglestone) Martin, my (Glenn Martin) father's mother, so that Ellen was my father's cousin. Ellen was a dressmaker, aged twenty-six; Siegfried was twenty-eight.

Despite his recent exposure as Baron von Einsiedel on a ship in Adelaide, Siegfried maintained the name of Hottelmann. It was his wish to leave the von Einsiedel name and title behind him. It was not until Siegfried and Ellen were together at the internment camp in 1942 that Ellen learned of the noble origins of her husband. Accordingly, this was not a factor in her relationship with him. A newspaper stated in February 1946, reporting on the internment inquiry: "A slim Sydney dressmaker married a German sailor, Siegfried Hottelmann, against her father's wishes in July 1939, and found, when she joined him in internment in 1942, that he was really Freiherr Siegfried Emil Heinrich von Einsiedel, a German baron, whose title is probably one of the oldest in Europe, dating beyond 1350."[12]

For Ellen, there was a possible disincentive to marrying Siegfried. Her father objected to the marriage, because Siegfried was German and Ellen's family was British. One document for the internment inquiry (Schedule 1) states, "In July 1939 he (Siegfried) married an Australian girl of British origin, apparently against the desires of her family".[13]

However, the assertion of British origin requires that, on Ellen's father's side, one goes back to her great grandfather, Peter Royall, who came to Australia from Norfolkshire around 1850.[14] On her mother's side, one also has to go back to her great grandparents, and two of those were convicts.

It was not the truth to say that Ellen was British, or that she married Siegfried against the wishes of her family. It was her father alone, Herbert Royall, who raised objections to the match.

It is clear that Herbert was against the marriage of his daughter to a German, but nothing is ever said about Ellen's mother's views, or those of her father's new wife. Moreover, one of the witnesses to the marriage is "D. Royall" This is Doreen, who was Ellen's sister, four years younger than Ellen. She was twenty-two, and was herself to be married in December 1939, to Gordon

Bowman. The other witness is A. Silverwood. The Births, Deaths and Marriages records indicate that this is Annie Silverwood, herself newly married (in 1939) to Thomas Silverwood.[15] This does not suggest that Ellen was lacking in support for her marriage to Siegfried. The support seems to be all around.

At the internment inquiry in February 1946, Siegfried said, "I did not exactly have some trouble with my father-in-law. I only met him once. He is English to the teeth and never met German people. To him, everything German was taboo. When I was there before we were married (at Herbert Royall's house), I was received very coolly because I was German. It did not worry us; we just got married. I have not spoken to hm since".[16]

The phrase "aristocratic nonchalance" comes to mind.

Siegfried and Ellen got married, but Siegfried did not have a stream of money coming to him from Germany, so he needed to work. He told Justice Simpson that he got a few odd jobs in this period. He said, "I also wanted to show that I got here on my own without help, and then that I could live on my own."[17] Although Siegfried sometimes compressed his accounts of events, so it is not clear exactly which year an event occurred in unless you know other factors, Siegfried told the inquiry: "I married on 1st July 1939. I was employed as a seaman on the steamer *Macedon* (managed by Howard Smith).... I remained with that ship for some time."[18]

The *Macedon* was on a regular route between Port Pirie, Melbourne, Sydney, Newcastle and Port Kembla, a round trip that generally took three to four weeks. It usually carried around 2,000 tons of coal and 2,000 tons of coke from Newcastle or Port Kembla to Port Pirie, then returned to Sydney via Newcastle, sometimes just carrying ballast. In the period August to October 1939, the *Macedon* was in Sydney on 17 August; at Newcastle 18 August, Port Pirie on 25 August, and on 30 August it was returning to Sydney via Newcastle.

6. September 1939: War is declared

Siegfried joined the ship either at Port Pirie around 25 August, or in Sydney around 30 August. Note that war was declared on 3 September, so Australia was, from that point on, part of the hostilities. One effect of this was that the shipping reports, of which there had been around a dozen per day in newspapers around Australia, reporting on the movements of hundreds of ships, suddenly ceased. The newspapers now had a responsibility to keep this information hidden from the view of the enemy.

Just at this point in time, 2 September 1939, at the beginning of a six-year world war, this piece appeared in a South Australian newspaper under the heading "Transport Assembly":

Cycling up from the Smelters [one of the wharves at Port Pirie] at noon the other day I saw something which I deem a phenomenon. A pair of draught horses were drawing a heavy trolly near International Hotel; a steam train from Adelaide was just pulling in; the steamer *Macedon* was swinging in the harbor basin; we were on our cycles; a motor truck was passing; and overhead the twin-engined mail 'plane was roaring southward. At first glance this may seem a small thing. But I venture to say that one might wait a lifetime and not again see the six graduated forms of transport thus assembled—all in motion simultaneously in their ordinary avocations.[1]

There is no relevance of this article to Siegfried's story; he may or may not have been on the *Macedon* at the time, but it leaps out as a comment on the passing of time at a critical juncture in human events.

In his interview at the internees' inquiry, Siegfried revealed more of his brief life in Australia at the start of World War II. He said that he played the role of a German officer in the film "Forty Thousand Horsemen".[2] This film was shot in Sydney between May and August 1940, at Bondi and Cronulla/Kurnell.[3] If Siegfried was in it (and I assume he was), it was as a minor character; he does not appear in the credits for the film.[4]

In an interview with a sergeant at Kogarah Police Station on 7 May 1940, Siegfried said that in two days' time he was going to be playing the part of a German officer in the film. A man named Charles Chauvel was making this picture film at the Cine Sound, Eveleigh St, Waverley.[5] The battle scenes were shot at Cronulla in July and August, using the 1st Light Horse (Machine Gun) Regiment and the 30th Battalion.

The film tells the story of the Australian Light Horse which operated in the desert at the Sinai and Palestine campaign during World War I. It follows the adventures of three rowdy heroes in fighting and romance. The film culminates at the Battle of Beersheba which is reputedly "the last successful cavalry charge in history". The film was clearly a propaganda weapon, to aid in recruitment and lift the pride of Australians at home during World War II. It was one of the most successful Australian movies of its day. The cast included Grant Taylor, Betty Bryant, Pat Twohill, and Chips Rafferty.[6]

Figure 12: Poster for the movie, "Forty Thousand Horsemen"

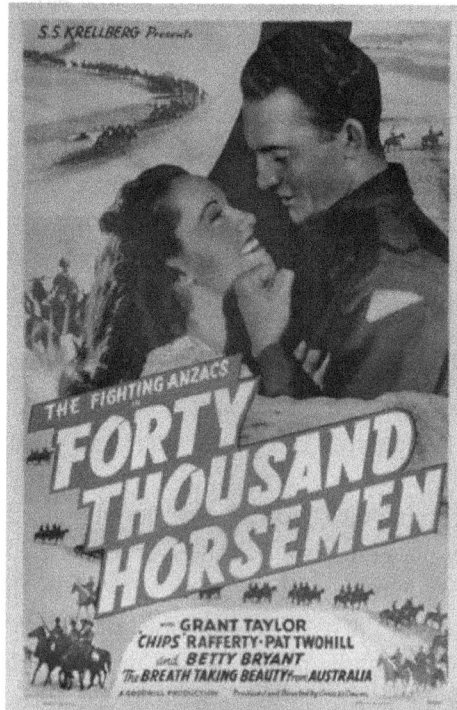

Where was Siegfried living during this time?

On 1 July 1939, the day they got married, Siegfried was living at 8 Springfield Avenue, Potts Point, while Ellen was living at the boarding house at 134 Forest Road, Arncliffe. On 6 September (just after war was declared), Siegfried had to report to the police station in Sydney, and in his statement he says that he is living with his wife at the boarding house in Arncliffe. The police records say that he was still there in March 1940, and another police report says he was there in May 1940 as well.

After the marriage, to gain work, Siegfried signed onto the ship, *S.S. Macedon*. This was managed by Howard Smith, for whom he had worked before, on the *Mungana*. The ship made regular trips around the Australian coast, so Siegfried was occasionally in Sydney.

On 26 September 1939, he visited the Rockdale Police Station and registered himself locally as an "Alien Resident in Australia". His address was 134 Forest Road Arncliffe, the boarding house where Ellen was living. His name is given as Siegfried Hottelmann, but also as Baron von Einsiedel. But this was not known to Ellen.

His height was five feet seven inches, he was medium build, with dark blonde hair and blue eyes. There is a photo attached to the form, a stately-looking photo with Siegfried wearing a dark suit and tie. The photo might have been one that Siegfried had been carrying with him from Germany, but more likely it was taken at the recent wedding.[7]

Figure 13: Siegfried Hottelmann, photo from police file

When the *Macedon* reached Sydney on 30 October 1939, he was paid off. He then got a job with a company called British Products as a salesman canvassing from door to door, but this only lasted a few weeks.

Siegfried told police he did not make a success of it. The sales manager, Mr H. Burrell, wrote a letter to the police several months later, saying that he sacked him because he took him to be a German and a "doubtful alien". Mr Burrell said that at the initial job interview, Hottelmann had told him he was a Canadian Finn (presumably because he had an American accent), not a German, although he could speak German fluently. However, one day Burrell had walked in on a conversation where Hottelmann was saying that Hitler was a great man, and it was only propaganda brought about by British people that made people think he was otherwise.

Burrell said in the letter: "Myself being a British and very loyal subject, I doubted the nationality of this man." After relaying the above conversation, he said that he had since learned that Hottelmann was travelling on a boat between Melbourne and Newcastle, inferring that this was suspicious: Siegfried might be spying.[8]

At the Internees' Inquiry in 1946, Justice Simpson asked Siegfried, "Did you ever say Hitler was a great man?"

Siegfried said, "I never said anything of that kind.... I believe we are really the one and same race and belong together."[9]

This was quite a revolutionary thing to say, particularly just at the end of the immensely destructive world war. He could have made any kind of statement about Hitler the man; he could have been defensive, or expressed a view about nationalism, yet he chose to say this: "we are really the one and same race and belong together".

Siegfried's greatest personal concern in 1940 was money. At this stage he was living at the boarding house at Arncliffe with Ellen. On 18 December 1939, he signed onto the *William McArthur*, a collier managed by the Howard Smith company. The ship had been built in Aberdeen in 1924, and was registered in Melbourne; it continued in service until 1961.[10] Siegfried was paid off in Newcastle on 13 January 1940 when he contracted blood poisoning in his arm. He was admitted to Iluka Hospital, Newcastle, and remained there for three weeks. Ellen went up to see him.

Figure 14: The William Macarthur

In doing so, Ellen happened to run into her former boss, Mrs Thauban. Ellen had not seen her for several months. Mrs Thauban had been the manager of a wholesale clothing manufacturing business in Dymock's building in George Street, Sydney, employed by a Mrs Lee, and Ellen worked there as a dressmaker or tailoress. In those days she was known as Nellie Royall. In the police record from Newcastle, we even learn that Mrs Lee is now the proprietor of the Rose, Shamrock and Thistle Hotel in Rozelle; this fact has no relevance to Ellen's story. Mrs Thauban visited Nellie in Newcastle after Siegfried was released from hospital, and thus she met him. The police report says nothing about this visit or about Siegfried.

However, the police had other information about Siegfried. Sister Yates, a nurse at the hospital, said that Nellie spoke very bad, broken English, but that Siegfried spoke good English. Siegfried had said he was born in Germany and he was an actor in America, where he was a naturalised subject. (There is no suggestion anywhere else that Siegfried was ever an actor in America, or that he was naturalised there. However, it could be noted that this was before Siegfried performed in the movie, "Forty Thousand Horsemen".) A later police report (17 July 1940) noted, "Although the (earlier) report refers to her as speaking very bad English, we might state that she speaks English very well and with an Australian accent only and nothing foreign about it".[11]

31

How does one explain Nurse Yates' observations? One would expect a nurse to be keenly observant. Perhaps it was the air of widespread suspicion that arises when a world war has been declared. But perhaps also, Siegfried was exerting his charm among strangers, and that can prompt people to jump to unexpected (and unwarranted) conclusions.

Siegfried went back to Sydney on 8 February, to the boarding house with Ellen. He kept in contact with the agent at Howard Smith, updating them with his current address, for he was hoping for more work on ships. However, the agent said he had received instructions from the Mercantile Marine Office on 30 January 1940 that he was not to issue a permit to Hottelmann to go to sea, given that he was German. But things are never simple; the agent told police that Hottelmann had been assigned to a ship from Sydney, not Newcastle.

Meanwhile, rumours about Siegfried were circulating. A Lieutenant-General G.S. at Army headquarters in Melbourne received a report from Naval Intelligence to say that Hottelmann had disappeared and that efforts should be made to "trace this man". He "is reputed to have won the Iron Cross while in the German submarine service during the last war".[12] A memo was sent to the Commonwealth Investigation Branch at Martin Place in Sydney in early March.

A subsequent police report in Sydney observed that "It is difficult to reconcile this (the idea of Siegfried being in the submarine service in World War I) because this man being born in 1911 he could not have been a member of the Naval service. He produced his passport".[13]

The "disappearance" related to his time on the *Macedon* and in the hospital at Newcastle. By now (March 1939) he was back at 134 Forest Road, Arncliffe. A policeman visited there in early May and interviewed Mrs Buckley, the keeper of the boarding house. Mrs Buckley stated "He is very well conducted, and by his conversations with the other boarders he appears to be a very loyal man towards the British Empire. I have known his wife for the last twelve years. Her maiden name was Ellen Mary Royall. I also know her mother and father, they are very decent people".[14] (Note, this would refer to the step-mother, Gladys.)

The report went on: "He has no associates other than the boarders at this address. He does not belong to the Communist Party, nor does he visit any foreign clubs. This man has no money and Mrs Buckley is allowing him and his wife to reside until he obtains employment". This was just before Siegfried was to start work on the "Forty Thousand Horsemen" film.

On 15 May 1940, Siegfried called in to see the police in Sydney. He volunteered the information that he had been a member of the Steel Helmet Organisation (Der Stahlhelm) in Germany. I think that Siegfried was politic in his disclosures, aiming to assure the authorities that he was no threat, and he was no fan of Hitler.

Der Stahlhelm was initially for veteran soldiers of the First World War, but in the late days of the Weimar Republic (the Weimar Republic was established at the end of the war after Kaiser Wilhelm II abdicated, but it collapsed in 1923) it was associated with the monarchist German National People's Party. It was revanchist, meaning that it aimed to recover territory lost in World War I, but it distinguished itself from the Nazi Party, and Hitler progressively forced it into subservience to the Nazi Party. Finally, he abolished it in November 1935.

In the same interview, Siegfried volunteered that whilst in Germany he had many discussions on the building of troop-carrying submarines and he felt that he owed it to his loyalty to Australia to convey this information to the British authorities. However, the police dismissed this information as being common knowledge, and they were of the opinion that Siegfried was seeking to mislead Military Intelligence. Nevertheless, it concluded: "He has not been interned" although "he is an enemy alien of military age". [15]

He obtained work on the *William McArthur* again on 16 May, but was terminated on 7 June 1940. The day before, there was a handwritten note in the Army's papers from Lieutenant Loughman addressed to Lieutenant Phillips, Ordnance, Mechanical Engineers, Victoria Barracks, stating that "Hoffman Siegfried is on a coal ship running between Newcastle and Melbourne. Hoffman is said to have a wireless set on his private boat which he says he cannot use except when at sea. He is very anxious to get back to South America. This man's wife is staying with relatives of Lieutenant Phillips. Do you want any further information on this man? If so, please let the writer know".[16]

This information is, at the least, garbled, and its source is not stated. The name is Hottelmann, not Hoffman. There is no mention anywhere else of him having a wireless set, and it seems merely fanciful to suggest he had a private boat. And Ellen is staying at a boarding house, not with anyone's relatives. The puzzling piece, however, is the mention of South America, as Siegfried's daughter reported that Siegfried had visited Brazil. Not that Siegfried confirmed this. Perhaps it was just talk.

Two weeks later (19 June), Navigation and Lighthouse Services sent a note to Military Intelligence:

Subject: National Security (Alien Control) Regulations – Aliens Employment Order, Re Hottelmann.

He was advised by me that he could not be issued with a licence (that is, to go to sea as a sailor) because he was not a British Subject. Notwithstanding this, he has made personal representations requesting that the matter be reconsidered. He claims that he married an Australian girl who is, within the next few weeks, to become a mother, and that he is known to the military authorities and claims that they refrained from interning him. An indication might be given as to whether there are reasons for recommending a variation of the decision already given by me.

Lieutenant Tyrrel pencilled in a response on the note: "Unless you have any view to the contrary, I propose to refuse the application". This was on 27 June 1940.[17]

On 28 June 1940, a man called Godfrey Englander called on the police with some information on Hottelmann: "Englander called, with info about Hottelmann, residing at Kelvin Court (this should say Kenton Court), Woolloomooloo. He is German, arrived 1938, seaman, pronounced Nazi. Married Aust girl, about to give birth. Said to be party leader in Hamburg".[18]

Englander called on the police again on 22 July 1940 with more information. He said Hottelmann was using the alias 'Hoffman', but his real name was von Einsiedel. He was living at 15 Kenton Court in

Cathedral St. He had a newborn daughter, and his wife was Australian. He has said "England started the war". The police recorded the comments and noted them as "questions to investigate".[19]

On 16 July 1940, Ellen attended Kogarah Police Station, registering as an "Alien resident in Australia". Ellen was registered as the "Australian-born wife of Siegfried Emil Hottelmann, an unnaturalised German". Her personal appearance was recorded and her fingerprints were taken, and there is a photo attached to the form. Ellen was just five feet tall, brown hair, slim build and hazel eyes. [20] This bears remarkable similarity to that of her great grandmother, Sarah Crosby, at her trial in London prior to her transportation to Van Diemen's Land in 1850.

Figure 15: Ellen Royall, from police file

On the same day, Siegfried attended the police station at Sydney and gave them an account of his history. The report notes that he arrived in Australia on 28 August 1938 (this is when the *Tisnaren* was in Melbourne). He is a seaman and rigger, and he is currently unemployed and in receipt of food relief. He stated that "he has no relatives employed in any factory or business engaged in production of munitions, war materials, equipment or uniforms for army, navy or air force. No relative in government employment."

He gave Mrs Buckley, of the boarding house at Arncliffe, as a reference. She was contacted and vouched for him. His associates were named as Mrs Bowman at Blakehurst, and Mr Price of Cronulla. (Ellen's younger sister Doreen had married Gordon Bowman; her older sister Daphne had married George Price.) The report continues:

"The value of his property is nil. Amount of cash: 1/2 (one shilling, two pence; no pounds). Cash at bank: nil. No driver's licence. Not a member of Fascist or Nazi party or any kindred organisation. Member of the Seamen's Union. Has never appeared in court in Aust or anywhere else.

"Mrs Buckley said he had conducted himself in a satisfactory manner. He did not hold parties or keep late hours, and was not visited by other foreigners. He was not known to the local police except as an alien reporting. He had not expressed any anti-British or subversive utterances or committed any subversive act.

"General remarks: He is at present living apart from his wife because he is German and his wife's people will not have him at their home. He answered all questions promptly and produced all papers necessary. Owing to the fact that he has travelled the coast of Aust we are of the opinion that action should be taken to restrict his movements. He states that he has no relative at present serving in the military, navy or air force in Germany.

"He is residing at Cathedral St in close proximity to Woolloomooloo wharves, so he should move.

"Signed, Constables Shirlaw and Lansdowne".[21]

The focus on Siegfried was becoming intense. On the following day, 17 July 1940, he was interviewed again, and his history was explored back to when he left school at fifteen (in 1926). Siegfried told the police about his visit to Australia in 1928, and his return to Germany. The facts he offers are selective; one might say inevitably so.

He said that on arrival in Germany he was refused any work and only stayed two months. The authorities told him to go back where he came from. (I don't know why the German authorities would have had this attitude towards him. In any case, we know that he lived in Hamburg and was issued a passport from there in September 1935.) He got a job as seaman on a ship to America. He stayed there about eighteen months. The police comment that "whilst there he appears to have acquired the American twang of speaking and speaks English fluently".[22]

The account Siegfried gave includes his times on board various Australian ships. He ends by saying he was on the "coastal steamer *Aeon*, and stayed with that ship until 24 May 1939. He was then paid off, and remained in Sydney for six weeks, during which time he got married, very much against the wishes of his wife's parents".

The police account continued, mentioning his role in the "Forty Thousand Horsemen" film. He was questioned as to his loyalty and he stated that he was with the British Empire, although he states that he returned to Germany for the purpose of staying there, but was not allowed to do so. (The first part of this statement may have been true when he returned (1930), but the latter assertion raises questions. Siegfried seems to have left Germany intentionally in 1936.) Others in the flats speak well of him, and nothing could be gained to establish that he is anti-British.

His wife, whose maiden name is Ellen Mary Royall, was born at Rockdale of Australian parents. She has not registered as an alien and when questioned regarding that matter, stated that when war broke out with Germany, she applied to the authorities to revert back to her Australian nationality, but has not received any reply to her application to date. She was advised to immediately register as an alien, which she said she would do as soon as she could. This woman is pregnant and expects a child to be born in about one week's time.

This report is signed by Detective Sergeant Samuel Sharp and Constable Waldock.

More talk about Siegfried came to the police. A Mr Armstrong of Blakehurst (which is where Ellen's younger sister, Doreen, lived) called at the police station two days later (19 July 1940). He said that "A German, who claims to be a Canadian Pole and whose name is not known except that the Christian name is Siegfried, had by his talk convinced Mr and Mrs Price (Ellen's sister and her husband), together with his wife and other people residing in the Cronulla district, of the justice of Hitler's cause, and of the fact that Aust would be much better off under Nazi rule."

Mr Armstrong said that Siegfried had a very domineering manner. He knew that Siegfried had acted in the movie, and that he had played the part of a German officer. He also said that Siegfried claimed to have made frequent trips between Australia and Germany, and he boasted of having been in the German secret police. Note, this report suggests that Ellen was staying at Blakehurst, which is where her younger sister, Doreen, was living with her husband, Gordon Bowman. Given that this was only a day before the baby was born, we can assume that this is where Ellen was living when the baby was born.

Two constables subsequently interviewed Mr and Mrs Price (her older sister, Daphne, and her husband George) at their residence "Rewa", Taloombi St, Gunnamatta Bay (incorrectly stated in the report as 'Paloombi'). The constables established that the man is Siegfried Hottelmann, and he is married to Mrs Price's sister. They stated that Hottelmann and his wife had resided with them for three or four days early this year, but he had never said or done anything to which exception could be taken, although the war question was often debated.

Figure 16: Kenton Court in Cathedral Street, Woolloomooloo

Mr and Mrs Price informed the police that Hottelmann and his wife were currently living apart owing to the fact that Mrs Hottelmann was shortly to be confined. Hottelmann was very much attached to his wife and had offered himself for internment so that his wife could be supported by the authorities.

Following this interview, two policemen called on Siegfried at Cathedral Street. Siegfried was forthcoming. He said that he was living there on his own in order to reduce expenses. His wife was living with her mother. (This was not quite true; she was living with her sister Doreen at Blakehurst. I don't know if she ever lived with her parents again after leaving home years earlier. She had left home when she was about fifteen, to live at Arncliffe in the boarding house run by Mrs Buckley.)

Siegfried further stated that he was unable to follow his usual occupation of seaman owing to restrictions on aliens of German origin. He showed a letter signed by F. Terry, Collector of Customs, South Australia and dated 1 March 1939 advising him that the Secretary of the Department of the Interior, Canberra had approved of him remaining in Australia permanently.

"Further particulars regarding Hottelmann can be obtained from his dossier and a report submitted by Constables Shirlaw and Lansdowne of this Section." The tone of this sentence is that the police have lost interest in the case. At this point, Siegfried had been interviewed five or six times. The baby, Sieglinde, was born on 20 July 1940.[23] It was Ellen's own birthday.

A further interview took place, on 26 July. The police asked him about his names:

> He said his correct name was Hottelmann, his father's. His father was an engineer on a large scale; he died in 1918. He was asked about von Einsiedel but he was very evasive in his answers. He admitted it was his grandfather's name and he was a baron. He had used the name in Germany but not since then.
>
> He is the only son of the family. When he went back to Germany in 1930, his people sent for him when he was at Hanover, and wanted him to take up his position amongst the aristocracy again. He states that his family

are pure-bred Germans of 700 years generation and that his grandfather the Baron as far as he knew up until 1938, was still in Germany with his family and alive.

He did not appear to want to talk about the name von Einsiedel, but on close questioning did finally admit that it was the family name, and was very much surprised to learn that the police had obtained that name, and we might add that he was fidgety and went pale-looking when being questioned on the subject.[24]

The two policemen concluded their account of the interview as follows:

This man owes the landlord of the flats where he is residing rent, and we are of the opinion that he will as soon as it is convenient for him to do so, leave this address, taken into account that his wife has just given birth to a child. Probably as he is an all-round seaman he will be hard to locate in the future, seeing that on two occasions he has stowed away on ships and on another occasion he deserted a ship in Sydney and has taken the alias of Hopps so as not to be detected as a deserter when in New Zealand.

Amusingly, Siegfried's young-man adventures from around 1930 have been interpreted as a lifelong tendency to stow away on ships and as a sailor, to be a deserter. I don't know of any evidence that he used the alias "Hopps"; he may have done so in New Zealand.

The "Summary of Personal Particulars" compiled by the Commonwealth on 29 July 1940 simplified things. It accepted all the items of information deemed to be suspicious, even where these had been discounted in subsequent interviews:

This man is viewed with grave suspicion. He is really the grandson of a German baron, and admitted this only under pressure. In May 1940 he claimed to be a Finnish subject, but his pro-Hitler conversation betrayed his attitude. Hottelmann was a party leader in Hamburg. Another informant stated that Hottelmann claimed to be a Canadian Pole, and that by his talk he had convinced neighbours (named) of the justice of Hitler's cause; that

Australia would be much better off under Nazi rule; that he made frequent trips between Australia and Germany; and that he boasted of having been in German Secret Police.[25]

Much of this statement seems to derive from the statements by Burrell of the British Products company. It is not clear what the mention of the German Secret Police refers to. Did it refer to the S.A., for example, or was it a complete fabrication?

7. Siegfried is interned

Immediate internment was recommended. Accordingly, on 2 August 1940, at 3:15 p.m., Siegfried was arrested at 103 Cathedral Street by Constables Hillier and Strachan, and taken to Long Bay Penitentiary. At this point, people are reduced to their rudimentary characteristics and their meagre possessions. His hair was fair; his eyes were blue. Distinctive marks? Moles on both the right and left cheeks. His height? Five feet six inches. We might find some humour in the variations in his basic description by different parties. His hair was anything from fair to dark brown; his height was anything from five feet six inches to five feet nine inches.

Siegfred's clothing consisted of one pair of pyjamas, one pair swimming trunks, two singlets, two pairs sox, two handkerchiefs, one pullover, one coat, one shirt, one pair slippers. His sundries included one toothbrush, one tin of tooth powder, one shaving soap, his passport and papers, a coat hanger, a fountain pen, one coat brush, eight packets of tobacco and eight packets of cigarette papers. And one fruit cake.[1]

From Long Bay he was taken to Orange, where a temporary internment camp had been set up in the cattle pavilions at the showground, and on 29 August he was transferred to Tatura in the north-east of Victoria.[2] Several internment camps were set up around Tatura, Rushworth and Murchison during World War II. Some of these were for civilians, and some for prisoners of war, with a capacity of more than 8,000 prisoners. The camps held many nationalities, as people were sent there not only from around Australia, but also from other countries that were part of the British Empire.[3]

8. Tatura internment camps

Note: The information in this section comes primarily from the book, *Marched In*, by Lurline and Arthur Knee, 2008.

Tatura Camp No. 1 was opened in 1940 and housed German and Italian internees.[1] The internment camps were located far from Australian cities and the coast, and the intent of the camps was that internees would not have contact with Australians. The men were initially housed in unlined huts, and more huts had to be built as internee numbers increased. The mess halls were the only heated rooms in the camp and during the colder months these were overcrowded.

Some of the first Germans to arrive in the camp were German wool-buyers who had been working in Australia for some years, employed by German firms. Since they travelled a lot in the course of their work, it was felt that their knowledge of the country, its road and rail networks and ports, would serve them well as spies for Germany. Some of those interned had spoken out brashly about their loyalty to Germany and their admiration of Hitler.

The Viennese Mozart Boys Choir was in Australia at the time war was declared. It was in Perth, about to board the ship to return to Austria. The boys were aged from eight to fourteen. The authorities were not clear what should be done with them. After the intervention of the Roman Catholic Archbishop Mannix, the choir was allowed to stay in Australia, the boys being billeted with parishioners in Melbourne. The conductor, Dr Georg Gruber, however, was interned in March 1941 and sent to Tatura. When an orchestra was established in the camp, he assumed the role of conductor.

Camp No. 1, to hold one thousand men, was constructed quickly. It was separated into two compounds. By January 1940 it had been completed to a stage where it could be occupied, and the first internees were marched the four kilometres from Dhurringile Mansion, where they had been temporarily housed. In February they were joined by internees who had been housed in gaols in Sydney, Bathurst and elsewhere in New South Wales, South Australia and Queensland.

Figure 17: Tatura Camp 1, 1943, showing division between compounds A and B

AUSTRALIAN WAR MEMORIAL   052408

The camp was roughly a rectangular area, surrounded by barbed wire and with six guard towers to keep watch on the prisoners. Generators provided power for the perimeter and search lights at night-time. The huts, which each held twenty-four men in one long, unpartitioned room, had corrugated iron external walls, and chicken wire instead of glass in the windows. Ventilation was via a run of chicken wire under the eaves. Initially the huts had no internal walls.

An infrastructure was established to organise guards, food and other services. Beds consisted of straw-filled palliasses and there was little furniture. However, the internees were enterprising, and gradually turned rubbish they found into tools and chairs, stools and bedside cabinets.

Camps 2 and 3 were opened in September 1940. By this time the war in Europe was intensifying, and the British government wanted to send up to 50,000 internees to Australia, to ease its own troubles. From one camp, then two, there were to be four camps, all in the Tatura district.

At different times, Camp 2 housed German Jewish internees, Italian prisoners of war and German officers. The huts in Camp 2 were divided into cabins. The cabins were small; they had a table and two chairs, two beds and a window. Bathrooms were clean but only one section had hot showers. Food was adequate and a Kosher kitchen was established for the Jewish internees.

Figure 18: Tatura Camp 1

Camp 1, viewed from the Garrison Quarters.

Camp No. 3 was for families. In the 1940-1941 period, internees had been brought to Australia from various places around the world: Britain, Palestine, Singapore, South Africa, New Guinea. Many of these people had been interned as families and then separated. At Camp 3, members of families were brought together again. The huts were divided into rooms, with twelve rooms in each hut, and there were four compounds.

However, different national groups were not separated, so there were Germans, Austrians, Italians all together, some of whom were Jewish. There were occasional disputes between the groups. Some of the Germans were Nazi sympathisers and they taunted the Jews. Some men regarded as troublemakers were shifted to a detention centre in South Australia. Eventually the compounds were better organised; Italian families were put into Compound A, German families from New Guinea were in Compound D. Otherwise, families with surnames from A to K were in Compound B, while families with surnames L to Z were in Compound C.

Over time, the Australian authorities realised that it was a mistake to have interned some of the men, and they were offered the choice of serving in the Army, either as soldiers or non-combatants.

As life in the camps settled down, internees sought to improve their lives. They were imprisoned, and there was no escape from that, but in other ways life was tolerable. Food was ample: plenty of meat, milk, butter, cheese and eggs. Internees and prisoners of war received the same food and accommodation as the Australian Army soldiers guarding them.

Figure 19: Tatura Camp 3; woodcuts of the camp, by Ludwig Hirschfeld-Mack

Families were encouraged to have vegetable gardens, and diligent gardeners grew tomatoes, sweet corn, strawberries, capsicum, zucchinis and watermelons. The kitchen was available each afternoon for anyone who wished to cook. Women carried on with the chores of housework: washing, ironing, mending, knitting and sewing.

Gradually, conditions improved, although materials were in short supply in Australia in these war years. The internal walls were lined and rooms had doors. Glass windows were installed. Officially there was no heating, but the men made heaters from four-gallon drums, lining them with concrete, and with little chimneys made from large tins soldered together. The Tatura area was freezing in winter.

Each compound had an elected leader, who was responsible for the efficient organisation of life in the compound. Many of the internees had been interned during World War I, and they knew it was important for people to have tasks to occupy themselves, and for them to be useful and productive. The kitchens, dining rooms, washrooms and other areas were cleaned daily. Responsibility for meal preparation and clean-up was assigned. Rooms were kept clean and tidy.

There were separate buildings for baths, showers and laundries. Water was heated in large wood-fired boilers. There were weekly rosters for washing clothes and using the clothes lines.

Those who had skills employed them and taught others. For example, one man was a shoemaker by trade, and he taught other men how to make sandals and fur-lined slippers (from sheepskins). Other men were wood-turners, leather-workers, jewellers and cabinet-makers. When clothes wore out, instead of being replaced, new material was given, and the women made up clothes from that. Old clothes were unpicked, cut up and re-sewn. Wool could be ordered from the canteen. It came in skeins, and had to be rolled into balls before knitting began.

Camp 3 included many children, and regular schooling was offered, making use of the many internees who had relevant skills, and in many cases, qualified teachers. Children were also expected to take part in camp chores, as appropriate to their age: starting with sweeping, and serving food. The Army supported the educational endeavours, such as by acquiring paper and pencils. The halls were used for lessons, then converted back to dining space for meal-times. Schooling went from kindergarten right through to senior secondary level.

The camps also conducted theatrical performances, organising, performing, and carrying out all the accompanying roles, including advertising the performances. There were many skilled performers and artists among the internees. Sports were also arranged. Tennis courts and "skittle alleys" were constructed, and athletics events were conducted.

9. Siegfried at Tatura

When Siegfried first reached Tatura, he was placed in Camp 1. For a time he was a member of the camp orderly service. However, he was concerned that wood and furniture were disappearing, being appropriated for personal creative projects. The Army required compensation for these stolen items. Siegfried feared that he would be ordered to engage in stealing items, so he quit from the role as orderly. He told the inquiry in 1946, "I could have been told, but I said I would like to take my leave in order that I would not be told".[1]

However, Siegfried's main concern at this time was the welfare of Ellen and their baby, Sieglinde. Siegfried had been in touch with his wife, and as her financial situation worsened, he suggested that she should request to be interned. In December 1940 he made an application for leave to submit objections against his detention order.[2] There was a process involving a tribunal to hear such applications. Presumably his intention was so that he could be reunited with his wife. However, the application was refused.[3]

After that, he worked at helping her to be interned with him. He pointed her to the Swiss Consul, which was intervening in such cases. The camp censors noted a letter he had sent to her at 5 View St Arncliffe in September 1941, wherein he told her to take what money she could get from them:

> I think it would be a good idea if you take all the money you can get from the Consul even if you don't need it so much at present. You would save it for a trip to Tatura...
> If any of that lady committee gets too nosy just tell them off and let them know that you are still a German citizen.
> If you get refused let me know and I will make a little stink from here....

This is quoted in a Conduct Report in February 1945 on Internee No. 1355 Hottelmann. The Camp Commandant had pencilled in the comment: "The Agitator type".[4]

Ellen agitated to join Siegfried, as many women agitated to join their husbands. On 15 December 1941, Lieutenant-General Powell, Eastern Command wrote to the Swiss Consul to say that consideration was being given to the internment of Ellen Hottelmann.[5] Ellen joined Siegfried in March 1942.[6]

A group of German women was sent to South Australia to be housed with families who had originally come to Australia from Germany, settling at Hahndorf, but the experience was difficult for them. The host families had been in Australia for generations, and they had been mistreated during World War I because of their background, so they were anxious not to be seen as German.

These women were the wives of Lutheran missionaries in New Guinea; their husbands were at Tatura. In a thoroughly modern fashion, they held a demonstration outside the local police station at Tanundra. Accordingly, the police arrested them. The ladies thanked the police. The demonstration had served to highlight the demand of the women, that they be interned with their husbands, and so they were, as Camp 3 had by now been constructed.[7] Ellen's reasons were somewhat different, but the concept of internment as a family group was well-accepted.

Years later, in February 1946 at the inquiry into the internees, Ellen gave her evidence to Justice Simpson about her circumstances in 1941. She said she was interned at her own request because of her financial difficulties. Siegfried supported her statement, saying, "My wife is very proud and would not ask anybody".[8]

10.Ellen joins Siegfried in internment

Ellen's registration card notes three changes of address between April 1941 and March 1942, all at Arncliffe. She was not living with her parents or her sisters. In a letter she wrote to Rose in 1945, she said "it is not wise to live with relations".[1] Perhaps her changes in address depended on how forbearing the property owner was about payment of rent or board. In March 1942 she was informed that she would be interned, and she handed herself in at Arncliffe on the sixteenth, with Sieglinde, by then eight months old. They were at first sent to an internment camp at Liverpool, then transported by train to Tatura, arriving on 20 March.

So began their life together under internment. There is a lack of records on Siegfried and Ellen over the next three years. Life in the camp goes on, with its routines and its diversions. But we know that it was when Ellen went into the camp that she first learned that her husband, Siegfried Hottelmann, was also Baron von Einsiedel, an ancient German family. In her ignorance, she could not have been accused of wanting to marry into nobility. And, additionally, the whole nature of German nobility was in flux, in these years of Hitler's Third Reich.

The hereditary title Baron von Einsiedel dates from the earliest days of the nobility. Nobility emerged in the Middle Ages (some titles had appeared before 1500), and grew in wealth, power and influence. It was a hierarchical system, with Barons ranking above Dukes and Counts. Barons would be comparable to a Baron of the English aristocracy. A Baron is called "Freiherr". The use of 'von' relates to the geographical origin of the noble family. Although some of the legal privileges of the nobility in Germany were abolished when the country became a Republic in 1919, German noble titles survived and were still respected.[2]

It seemed that Siegfried wanted to be an ordinary man, and that he had found a beautiful woman in Sydney and fallen in love with her, regardless of his poor circumstances, even regardless of the antipathy of her father. Siegfried did not seem to hanker for prominence in public or social life. His brief bout as an orderly in Camp No. 1 indicated that he was enterprising and innovative – he had an enthusiastic and inventive mind – but he would withdraw from social situations at the first indication that he would be pushed where he did not wish to go.

Nevertheless, Siegfried could give the appearance of readiness to lead, because he was well-educated and an easy conversationalist. A conduct report on internees carried out in February 1945 said:

> Hottelmann impresses as having held some social status and as having been well educated. He has been well-behaved during internment and apart from his signing the above letter (advising his wife to take what money she could; this was in 1941) and his being in receipt of the Reichstreue (German pocket money), he has given no indication of his political partialities during internment.[3]

A Conduct Report in March 1944 observed that Siegfried associated with Germans in A Compound of Camp No. 3. However, "Known remarks showing outlook, leanings: Nil. Statements of other internees about Siegfried: Nil. Any known acts: Nil".[4]

Despite these favourable observations in the Conduct Report, the camp authorities have collected a considerable file on Siegfried, and none of it goes away, even the parts that have been demonstrated to be false. Even his first visit to Australia in 1928 is taken as evidence against him. The Intelligence Officer's comments say, "Previous residence Australia 1928-30. Member of storm troopers in Berlin. Leading member of community (Nazis) on coastal shipping." A further comment has been added: "There is no evidence he has changed his opinions since his internment", although the Camp Commandant comments: "The internee and his wife have a good camp record".[5]

So, even being quiet is damning: "There is no evidence he has changed his opinions...." The reference to him being a member of the storm troopers in Berlin is not supported by any other police or security reports. Further, there is no mention of Siegfried ever having been in Berlin, and certainly not living there. There is mention of "storm troopers" among the reports on Siegfried, and this may be worthy of examination.

Siegfried accepted the Reichstreue, "pocket money" sent to internees by Germany (the word means loyal, faithful).[6] Siegfried was clearly pragmatic in these matters. He would not have refused to accept the money as a matter of principle. He seemed to have no other sources of income. There are a couple of times when the camp records mention his financial status. On 9 March 1944 his credit at the Commonwealth Bank was three pounds, fifteen shillings and two pence. On 1 February 1945, his credit at the bank was nil.

However, it was also important that people could be productive, and Siegfried started an initiative for the knitting of belts (macrame). He told the inquiry that he "worked that up efficiently" and he had a process ready to be patented.[7] The current Tatura Museum has some knitted items in its collection that were donated by one of his daughters. One suspects that Ellen's dressmaking skills were a contributing factor to this enterprise.

Figure 20: Knitted items for Tatura internees' enterprise

At the end of 1943, and into 1944, Siegfried was quite unwell. He had chronic dyspepsia. He was diagnosed with a duodenal ulcer and put on a special diet. He spent some time in the hospital, now called the Waranga Hospital.

A hospital had been set up in Camp 1 in December 1941. The Matron appointed was Beatrice "Trix" Moore, who had joined the Army and served at Puckapunyal Army Camp. She was told to go to Tatura and open a hospital. The hospital initially consisted of several galvanised iron huts to make four long wards, along with administrative offices and ablution blocks, all connected with a covered walkway. Equipment was provided, but conditions were basic. Matron Moore pressured the Army to improve conditions, and a morgue was added, a sterilising room, and as children were being born, a room to dry nappies.

The camps expanded, and prisoners were arriving from tropical parts of the world, so there were tropical diseases, infectious diseases, and diseases no one had had any experience of. Matron Moore, in an interview about the internment camps, said there was not much trouble with the patients, who were a mixture of internees and prisoners of war. However, she said that in the beginning, in 1942, some of them were "a bit arrogant", but she remembered "there was one particular man, a German from Hamburg, he ruled all the internees if they got a bit out of hand with the staff, he would bring them to order. They were a bit surprised".[8]

Matron Moore distinguished this man from the German officers, who were at first kept at a separate property, Dhurringile. They only turned up if they were coming in for treatment. She described them as being "a bit superior, and looked down their nose at us". So, we are left to wonder if the German from Hamburg was Siegfried. It is not difficult to imagine. From what we know about him from the records, he was imbued with what the author Dina Nayeri calls "aristocratic nonchalance".[9] He could assume, on necessity, a natural authority, and he did not need to hold onto that persona all the time.

In April 1944 the camp authorities were giving consideration to the release of a number of internees on medical grounds. Siegfried was among them. The difficulty was, in most cases, that the internees did not have any accommodation or employment in the community. The allied issue was that some internees were given consideration to be placed in the Civil Aliens Corps.

Members of the Civil Aliens Corps were required to work on projects of a non-combatant nature managed by Allied Works Councils in all states and the Northern Territory. These included projects such as road construction, or the forestry industries. If Siegfried was accepted into the corps, the problem of accommodation for his wife and child would still need to be solved.

However, the Director-General of Security (William Simpson) in Canberra received the medical report on Siegfried, and realised that he was not fit for the Civil Aliens Corps. He stated that if his release from the camp was approved, other work would be found for him by the Manpower Authorities. And the Director-General acknowledged that accommodation for his wife and child would still need to be arranged.[10]

On 10 May 1944, Siegfried was interviewed, and the report to the Director-General was that he had been in hospital with an ulcerated stomach, the medical officer had put him on a special diet, and Siegfried could not arrange accommodation in the community.[11] I think that Siegfried may have been feeling despondent at this time, wondering what would become of him and Ellen and Sieglinde.

A few days after this interview, a message was sent from Tatura Internment Camp No. 3 to the Consul for Switzerland, for the purpose of informing Germany. It listed the names of the men who had said they were unwilling to work in Australia. Most of the men had signed; it included Siegfried. The camp authorities intended to interrogate all internees now, to determine who wished to be repatriated to Germany after the war.[12]

Director-General Simpson writes to the camp, expressing the view that "there seems no alternative but to allow the family to remain interned. Please enquire into the prospects for their repatriation to Germany". The Deputy Director of Security in Melbourne writes back to confirm that Siegfried has been in Waranga Hospital for an ulcerated stomach, and they do not desire release. He says that the question of "their repatriation to Germany should be explored".[13]

The question muddles on. In July 1944 the camp is giving consideration to destitute internees. The Little Sisters of the Poor have been consulted. They had considered work for the Hottelmanns. They concluded that they could get work under the Manpower Authority at restaurants or hospitals.[14] Siegfried's dossier is shuttled back and forth between Tatura, Melbourne and Canberra.

It describes him as a Reichdeutsche. This is an archaic term (meaning German of the Reich, after its formation in 1871), but it probably signifies the fact that Siegfried held a German passport. It is not an indicator of Nazi sympathies. However, his knowledge of the Australian coast as a seaman is still held in suspicion. Even his stint as an elephant handler with Wirth's Circus in 1929 is described as being "engaged on the transport side of Wirth's Circus and at one period travelled with it through both New Zealand and various States of Australia".[15]

11. Associates in the camp

The dossier also reports on Siegfried's associations in the camp. Only two people are mentioned: "Associates in camp: No. 1058 Frerck, J who was a member of the Inner Ring in New South Wales, but who has been quiet during internment. He also appears friendly with No. 1206 Picker, F who has expressed Nazi sympathies but who has been well-behaved." The dossier notes that Siegfried "impresses as being well-educated and to have held some social status. Has given no indication of his political sentiments other than in the letter sent to Ellen in 1941".[1]

Johannes Frerck and Fritz Picker were quite different men, but they had some things in common, apart from being German. Both men were about thirty years older than Siegfried. When he went into internment, Siegfried was around thirty years old. His own father had died when he was only about seven, and his mother just two years later. When a young man becomes a father, it reminds him of his own family, and if it was wanting, it makes him sensitive to the presence of other models of fatherhood. Perhaps this was what Siegfried found in the two men.

Added to this tendency, institutional life does interesting things to people. It narrows the range of people available for interaction, and at the same time it increases the time available for interaction. Some spend that time talking about world affairs and politics; others take up a craft or hobby, or gardening, theatre, reading, or teaching. Some talk about the distant past. On this score, the two men offered different perspectives on the world.

Frerck and Picker had played different roles in the pre-war world, but the camp had put an end to all of that life. And also, the camp was a place of surveillance. Frerck and Picker, being older men, exercised caution. So, they were reported as being well-behaved.

Both Frerck and Picker had wives with them in internment, and both men had children, although their children were older than Siegfried's, and the family situations were quite different. Johannes Frerck and his wife Elsa had a daughter, Elsbeth, born in 1929. Elsbeth was in the camp with her parents.

Fritz Picker and his wife Marianne had one daughter in Australia: Waltraut, born in 1921. She was old enough to live independently, and she was not interned. But they had another two children. A son, Hennig was born in about 1924; a daughter, Heide, was born in 1926. Just before the war started, the parents had taken Hennig and Heide back to Germany and left them there so they could finish their schooling.

Marianne proudly told the authorities in 1941 that in Germany they would become "thoroughly Germanised, as she and her husband had the intention of returning permanently to Germany. Her son was a member of the Hitler Youth Movement and her daughter belonged to the Bund of German Girls". During the war, Marianne said, Hennig became a Lieutenant in the Army, and Heide joined the Red Cross.[2]

The family had lived in Fiji for a few years, and it seemed that Fritz had little desire to go back to Germany, but Marianne agitated to do so. They had taken up British citizenship in Fiji, but this was revoked in 1941 because of the war against Germany, and because they had moved to Australia. Fritz had been a porter at a hotel. In Sydney, Marianne ran a café in Hunter Street, La Morada.

Figure 21: Johannes Frerck

Johannes Frerck and his wife were far more publicly active. In the 1930s, he was said to be the Number Two Nazi in Australia (a Dr Becker was Number One), and he was proud of it. He was the

56

secretary of the New South Wales branch of the Nazi Party, and gave speeches at German events. In daily life he ran a delicatessen in William Street, Kings Cross. Could Siegfried have met him when he lived briefly in Springfield Avenue, Kings Cross?

Frerck came to Australia to live in 1926. He played an important part in the Nazis' "harbour system", visiting every German ship which arrived in Sydney and taking the sailors on picnics "to keep them out of the city and away from Communistic influences".

In May 1934, five hundred people in Sydney turned up for the commemoration of Germany's National Day. In his speech, Mr. J. Frerck, leader of the Sydney Nazis, said that the prophecy made in 1919 that Germany could not survive the effects of the war, had been averted by Hitler taking power. "We want to live in peace with every other nation," added Mr. Frerck, "but we cannot do it unless Germans everywhere have faith in their leader." A programme of national songs was sung, including "Deutschlandlied" and the Nazi song, "Horst Wessel".[3]

In 1936, the *Truth* newspaper "called on him in his shop, among the leberwurst, the smoked ham and the pickled herrings". He was quite frank about his influence as a Nazi: "I make reports to Berlin when I consider they are needed", he said.[4] In December 1938, two hundred people (described as Communists) picketed his shop, urging a boycott and shouting "Throw Frerck out of Australia! We don't want Nazi spies here".[5] A few days later there was another demonstration, and two women were arrested for offensive behaviour: handing out leaflets and shouting, "Don't buy from him. He's a member of Hitler's party, and Hitler is a murderer".[6]

On 3 September 1939, the United Kingdom declared war on Germany. When the news was known in Sydney, an empty beer bottle was flung at Frerck's shop window. It fell short, and smashed on the footpath. A few hours later a stone was thrown, and one of the glass panels of the door was broken.[7]

The same night, police and military officers interned nearly 300 aliens, many of whom were taken from their beds. Herr John Frerck was among them.[8]

After the war, at the internment inquiry, Frerck was interviewed by Justice Simpson and questioned about a notebook of his that had been found. It contained the names of many internees, with a code of marks against the names, and comments: untrustworthy, Communist, good for nothing, wife Jewish. He claimed not to remember what the marks meant, and that the book was just for his personal use, "in case I met some of those crooks later on, then I should know straight away that they could not take me down".

Did the words Frerck used in the speech in 1934 come back to haunt him ("We want to live in peace with every other nation")? Or were those words used in pure cynicism at the time? Frerck and his wife were deported to Germany. Picker and his wife had asked to be repatriated to Germany, but when the moment came and a ship was available, they turned the opportunity down. They had even packed their trunks for the journey. Ultimately, they remained in Australia.

12. Considering post-war life

In December 1945, the Conduct Report on Internee No. 1355 Hottelmann simply notes that he had made no application for release. In July 1945, Siegfried had typed a letter to the Camp Commandant:

> I previously expressed my desire to return to Germany. However, at the end of the war in Germany and the conditions under which I would have to live in my home country with my wife and two small children, have created entirely different aspects. I beg to submit my respectful regret, therefore, Sir, to kindly inform the competent authorities, that I do not want to avail myself anymore of the eventual possibilities of being repatriated to Germany but would prefer to stay in this country permanently when my internment terminates.
>
> I am particularly anxious to be granted these privileges in as much as my wife is a born Australian and both children were born in this country. Yours respectfully, Siegfried Hottelmann.[1]

A second child had been born on 26 February 1945, Ellen Waltraud Hottelmann, in Waranga Hospital. There is a photo in the Australian War Memorial collection of Siegfried, Ellen, Sieglinde and baby Ellen as a family group. In the latter days of the war, as the ominous mood of the early days eased, curious incidents like this occurred. A photographer was sent to the camp to record photos of families. It seems to have been done in the interests of history or posterity. The baby was just three weeks old.[2]

It is interesting that the baby's middle name was Waltraud. This was the name of Fritz and Marianne Picker's daughter, the one who was grown up and lived in Melbourne. The other family in the picture, the Dannenbergs, had lived in Australia for several years. Heinrich Dannenberg had been a wool-buyer.

Figure 22: Hottelmann family photo with Dannenbergs

Back row: Siegfried Hottelmann and Heinrich Dannenberg; *Front row:* Sieglinde, Ellen (mother) with baby Ellen, Hildegard Dannenberg, Maria Dannenberg

Did the arrival of another child help to shift the balance for Siegfried, from the desire to go back to Germany to the desire to remain in Australia? It is surprising that Siegfried wanted to go back to Germany anyway. When he deserted ship in Adelaide in 1938, it seemed to be evidence of a decision to stay here permanently, and not to go back to Germany. Of course, the fact that the country was in the control of the Nazi Party would have been a factor in his decision. And perhaps the Germans held in the internment camp thought that the war was going to result in the ousting of Hitler, so it might be worth going back there. And perhaps Siegfried was swayed by the conversation of his German compatriots.

Siegfried seemed to vacillate about whether or not to choose to go back to Germany. At the internment inquiry in early 1946 he said that in 1941, when Germany was having its greatest successes, he stated that he wanted to stay in Australia. In February 1945, he said he was willing to go to Germany. It was in March 1945 that he told the Intelligence Sergeant that he wanted to stay in Australia.[3]

At the same time that Siegfried was undergoing these turbulent changes of mind, the authorities were beginning to consider what would happen to the internees and prisoners of war at the end of the war. The Australian authorities accepted the provisions of the Geneva Convention. It provided that prisoners of war were to be returned to their home countries. The same did not apply to internees. Australia wanted migrants, and most internees chose to stay.

Most of the prisoners of war, Germans and Italians, were repatriated to their home countries, although it was a long process because of the shortage of shipping. Internees generally had a choice about their destination, either to stay or to return to where they had come from. Because there were many different types of groups at the Tatura camps, there were many possible answers. The internees' inquiry addressed the more difficult questions. In some cases, it was not possible for internees to return to where they had come from. For example, a group of Germans had come from Palestine, and the British had handed the land over to the Jewish people after the war, to form the new Israel. Germans were not welcome there.

Germans who had lived in Australia prior to the war could generally go back to where they had lived, if that were possible. It was necessary for internees to obtain employment and accommodation before they could be released from the camp. This was a vexed issue for Siegfried and Ellen, and one that was ongoing right to the end of their stay in the camp.

The censors at the camp read all the letters that were sent outwards and inwards, and copied parts they thought were relevant to security. In April 1945, Ellen wrote to her sister, Rose Stuart:

> Rose dear, I believe I am homesick to see you again, but would not let Siegfried know for the world. He did not go with the last repatriation but may go with the next. But should you girls [the three sisters, Daphne, Rose and Doreen] be able to find me a small flat or furnished rooms I am not fussy anymore, I am sure he would come with me instead, you can imagine how much more happier it would be for me after so long. I don't think I am asking too much, but Rose, it is not wise to live with relations again do you think? Siegfried does not know of

this, but he would not refuse me if he knew we had somewhere to go.[4]

Ellen worried about the impact of life in the camp on Sieglinde's later life. In November 1944 she wrote to Doreen: "I cannot imagine how most things will react on Sieglinde and us too after the war. The life here is very monotonous, and sometimes I just can't think to write a letter properly."

Figure 23: Sketch of Tatura Camp 3 by C. Gluckner

Siegfried's views on where to live after the war seem to have been bound up with his views about the direction of world affairs. He began to express his ideas publicly. His record includes these comments: "He feared the Russians and believed that Germany should align herself on the side of Great Britain – he had so advised other internees. There was a difference of opinion in the compound as to which side Germany should be on – that of Great Britain or with Russia."

A comment on 28 May 1945 says: "His wife was born in Australia and correspondence has shown that she has persuaded him to change his mind about repatriation. They have decided to remain in Australia and not accept repatriation to Germany if the question is again referred to them. In the meantime they are seeking a home in Sydney".[5]

13. Release from internment

However, Siegfried and Ellen were stuck. Siegfried had no means of income, given that during the war he would not be accepted as a sailor: he was German and held to be suspicious. And they had no home in the Australian community. The only hope was that one of Ellen's sisters could find a place for them. Siegfried did not seem to be associated closely enough with any other Germans in the camp to have discussed possibilities or considered collaboration with them.

Most of the Germans who had been wool-buyers before the war decided to stay in Australia, but many of them did not find their transition back into the community easy. Their previous positions were not available. One of them had married an Australian woman before the war, and she went back to her parents' farm. When the husband joined them after the war, he started a business buying day-old chicks and growing them on for sale. Later, he went to Sydney and started his own wool-buying business.[1]

During internment, was Siegfried reconsidering whether he should return to Germany after the war and take up his role as Baron von Einsiedel? There comes a point when a young man sees himself growing older, and rebelliousness starts to look like an indulgence. One has to look at what one's responsibility is in the world. And Siegfried's position was sitting there waiting for him, and him alone. Was it he who shouted at his fellow Germans in the hospital? Did he realise in that moment how naturally it came to him? And then how necessary it might be for him to take up this path? And how easily Ellen could become part of that life, too?

The idea of Baron von Einsiedel was not buried. People in the camp knew about it. We know this, because it was when Ellen came to the camp that she found out about this other side of Siegfried's life. One wonders what it meant to her, and what she felt. Australians know the story about Mary Donaldson, an advertising executive from Tasmania, meeting a man called "Fred" at Darling Harbour in September 2000 and liking him, before subsequently being told that he was the crown prince of Denmark. But that was just after they met, long before they married and eventually became the King and Queen of the country.

But Ellen was already married and they had one child when she found out. And then Siegfried would have had to explain to her how he had rejected the title and fled the country, fleeing one of the oldest families in Germany. Mary Donaldson accepted the challenge: to become a member of one of the oldest monarchies in Europe. She moved to Copenhagen, converted to the Lutheran Church and began studying Danish. Likewise, Ellen would have seen herself as potentially poised on the cusp of momentous change.

There is no doubt that other people saw the significance of Siegfried's position and Ellen's position. Siegfried's interview with Justice Simpson at the internees' inquiry was prefaced with the statement: "This man's real name is Baron von Einsiedel; but it appears that he attempted to hide from everyone, including his wife, the fact that he was of ancient lineage".[2]

Figure 24: Justice William Simpson

Justice Simpson knew of Siegfried Hottelmann. Back in March 1944 his case had come before him when he was the Director-General of Security. He had determined then that Siegfried was no security risk, and meant to release him then. However, messages had got muddled, and Siegfried understood that his release would be on the basis that he joined the Civil Aliens Corps, and Siegfried felt that he was unfit for such work. However, Simpson said he had accepted at the time that Siegfried was unfit for work with the Civil Aliens Corps. (Nevertheless, it seems clear from Siegfried's file that the remaining stumbling block was that Siegfried and Ellen could find nowhere to live.)

Justice Simpson begins his interview with Siegfried by asserting: "I have not the slightest hesitation in recommending that he should not be deported and that he should be released together with his wife and children at the earliest possible moment".[3]

What followed was a public interrogation by Justice Simpson of Siegfried's stance towards his noble family. It seems to have been conducted with an almost fatherly appeal for him to consider his position deeply.

"Your title is translated as Baron?"

"Yes. There are two kinds of Freiherr in Germany. One is the ancient title that dates before 1350. That is equivalent to the English Baron. The other Freiherr is called Baron in Germany but is equivalent to the English Baronet and they do not come into the peerage. We have seven pointers in our crown (coronet), the same as the English Baron.

"My father was killed in the last war, and when I went to school I was interned in the school. There are not many of them (internment places) in Germany, but it was because I was orphaned in Hamburg. I read books about adventure and decided I would go to sea. The only way I could get in a ship without anybody spotting me was by using the name Hottelmann.

"My father was an engineer. He built in 1911 the biggest dam in Europe. My mother died two years after my father. The law of inheritance is different in Germany to what it is in England, where the nearest male relative succeeds to the title. My grandfather adopted me so that the name would not die.

"Therefore it was easy to get papers in the name of Hottelmann. I got on a ship to Australia. I visited a German ship in Port Pirie, and there was my grandfather's gardener's son as an electrician and he recognised me. There were refugees on that ship. The ship went to Java and from Java to Australia, and they doubtless went straight to the police and told them about me."

Justice Simpson asked, "Don't you want to be known as Baron von Einsiedel?"

Figure 25: Map of the states of Germany

Siegfried answered: "I overthrew myself with my family because I had different ideas from them, and I wanted to go to Australia again. I was here as a boy of sixteen years. I was assistant scout master in the Sea Scouts and first instructor at Port Adelaide. I also wanted to show that I got here without help, and then that I could live on my own."

Justice Simpson: "You came to Australia first in 1928 and you stayed until 1930?"

Siegfried: "Yes. I worked as a farm hand and as a seaman."

"And for a while you were with Wirth's Circus as an elephant driver?"

"Yes."

"What do you know about elephants?"

"I do not know anything, but I wanted to see the world and I was prepared to work my way. I toured New Zealand with Wirth's Circus."

"Then you went back to Germany on a German ship?"

"Yes. I joined the S.A. in Germany. I finally came back to Australia in August 1938 by the ship *Tisnaren*, from which I got a landing permit and took my discharge. I never handed over my S.A. documents to the German Consul in 1939. I showed them at the Consulate and that is all. I handed over no documents. I married on 1st July 1939. I was employed as a seaman on the steamer *Masson* (*Macedon*), for Howard Smith. There were other Germans who were members of the crew. I remained with that ship for some time. I reported to the police on 6th September 1939.

"I was not interned until August 1940. Before internment, I played the part of a German officer in the film 'Forty Thousand Horsemen'."

Siegfried continues with his history. When he was interviewed by the police prior to internment, he said he did not conceal his correct name, but merely said "Here is my passport". He told them von Einsiedel was his grandfather.

"My wife was interned with me in 1942. She made application through the Swiss Consul. She was in considerable financial difficulty. In 1943 I suffered from a duodenal ulcer, but the Mixed Medical Commission did not recommend me for repatriation. There was a suggestion that I should be released early in 1944. It is not correct that my wife and I refused to be released because we were unable to find accommodation.

"In 1941 I applied to be heard before a tribunal but was refused. In 1944, after I was happy with my wife, a Sergeant came to Waranga hospital of which I was an inmate and said, 'You are to be released to go into a labour corps. We will give you 14 days' leave to find accommodation for your wife.' At that time everybody thought it was to go to Alice Springs and because of my ailment I thought it was ridiculous for me to go to such a place. I wrote to the authorities a letter of which I produce a duplicate."

Justice Simpson said, "What are we going to do with you? How are you going to earn a living?"

And Siegfried said, "That is easy."

Simpson continued, "Since March 1944 the Security authorities have been willing to release you if the problem of what to do with your wife and children could be solved."

"They never told me so." Siegfried explains how he started an industry for the knitting of belts when he was in Camp No. 1, and he had a process to be patented. He was a member of the seamen's union and he was not afraid of hard work, and if other avenues failed, he could go to sea. This evokes the story of the von Einsiedel relative who was working in a factory in America in 1930, looking to form the basis of an industry for his estate in Germany: an entrepreneur.

After Siegfried's interview is finished, Ellen is interviewed. She introduces herself as: "Ellen Mary von Einsiedel. I was married as Hottelmann. I did not know my husband's correct name when we were married. I was married in July 1939. I did not retain my British nationality on marriage. I have heard my husband's evidence. I agree with it and desire to be released in Australia. I think my sister can find us accommodation.

"I was interned at my own request because of financial difficulties. As to whether my parents would not assist me at that stage, there was no room; they had a very small cottage. My mother and father have both died since I have been interned, also my brother, which did not help me much either".

With this simple statement, Ellen underlines one of the tragedies of war: both her parents had died during the war, and she was unable to be there. Perhaps even more so because there was trouble between them over Siegfried, it would have been better if she could have been at their funerals. Perhaps some kind of peace could have been forged. There had been much trouble in the family in the past. The mother she was referring to who died was her step-mother, Gladys Alma, who died on 21 February 1944, aged forty-seven.[4] Her father, Herbert Augustus Royall, died on 30 June 1945, aged sixty-six. The cause of death was cerebral haemorrhage, arteriosclerosis, and hypertension.[5]

Ellen's brother George had died in 1942.[6] He had gone to Melbourne to live; he had married, and he died there, aged thirty-one. Her birth mother died in 1950.[7] I do not know if Ellen had any connection with her. Her correspondence from the camp was with her sisters.

Mr Justice Simpson told the baroness it was a misunderstanding that Siegfried thought he would be sent to Alice Springs, in case she should be bitter in the future about her internment. "You will be out of this place soon – I hope," he added.

The interviews with Siegfried and Ellen were considered very newsworthy, and they were reported in numerous newspapers across Victoria, New South Wales and Queensland. The articles note that at the inquiry, Ellen "was referred to as Freifrau and Baroness".[8]

One wonders whether Justice Simpson had read the application Siegfried made in December 1940 to contest his internment. The application was refused. However, there were parts of Siegfried's responses to the questions that would have brought interesting comment.

One question was whether any restrictions were placed on the applicant when he left Germany. Siegfried responded, "I just left as seaman." Understated but poignant.

Another question was about the applicant's reasons for departure. Siegfried said, "shang of Klimat".[9] This is the only occasion on which I have found Siegfried's English expression to be odd, but the meaning is clearly "change of climate". It is deeply ironic.

14. Seigfried's involvement in organisations

Some of Siegfried's statements to Justice Simpson invite further examination. I don't doubt, for the most part, that things happened if Siegfried said they happened. His life was full of adventure, which had its own driving logic, but that very logic should make us question some things. At the internment inquiry, he said he had been the Assistant Scout Master in the Sea Scouts at Adelaide for a time. In the context in which he says this, straight after saying he was here as a boy of sixteen, it sounds as if it happened on his first trip to Australia. But he was not in Adelaide when he deserted from the *Gustav*; he was in Melbourne, and from there he got a job on a farm in Victoria.

However, when he deserted ship in 1938, he was indeed in Adelaide, and for the first two months he was there, there is no record of what he did. And perhaps, spending time with some eager youths teaching them nautical skills while he was trying to figure out what to do next, would have been very inviting to him. He certainly had the sailing experience to impart from his voyage on the *Gustav*, as well as his experience on large ships crossing the oceans.

Perhaps talking about being in Australia as a sixteen-year-old prompted Siegfried to think about youngsters, and hence he talked about the Sea Scouts. It wasn't as if he was talking to try to cover up a crime; rather, he was describing the adventures of his innocence.

It may even have been contacts that he made through the Sea Scouts that led to him getting the job on the dredge. Would Siegfried have known about the Sea Scouts? Quite probably. The scouting organisation was founded in Britain by Baden-Powell in 1910, but it blossomed in other countries too, and sea scouts were a form of scouting from the start.

Germany had a Boy Scouts movement at the same time, and there were several similar organisations, such as Pfadfinderen and Wandervogel.[1] They conducted activities like hiking and camping, they taught associated skills, and they wore uniforms. Some of these organisations promoted "traditional" values, some were rather militaristic, some were more defiant of authority, and some were more back-to-nature orientated and less nationalistic. They continued after the First World War and were active during the

1920s, but when Hitler came to power in 1933, all of these groups were abolished, and youths had to join the Hitler Youth.

So, yes, Siegfried was very likely to have known about the Sea Scouts, and to have understood their place in society, particularly as all such groups in Germany had been banned after Hitler's take-over. But do we know if Siegfried was ever in the Scouts himself, or a variation of it, such as the Wandervogel? We know that after the death of his parents he lived in Hamburg, but we do not know very much about his life at that time, just that he was in school and he read books about adventure. The way he refers to school, relating it to internment, it sounds like a boarding school. He was, after all, to inherit the title of Baron. We know there was a conflict with his grandfather and he left Germany on the ship *Dresden* in December 1927, aged sixteen.

It is possible that he had been in a scouting group. If so, and he had seen a sign for the Sea Scouts in Adelaide in 1938, he would have been instantly attracted. But even if he had not been in the scouts, he would have understood the nature of what they were.

Figure 26: Australian Sea Scouts in 1930s

There is another statement that Siegfried only made once, at least as far as the records are concerned, and he made this statement at the inquiry. He said, "I was in this country when a child and nearly became a member of Toc H. I believe we are really one and the same race and belong together".[2] We can take this to mean when he was sixteen, in early 1928. But what was Toc H?

Toc H was an abbreviation for Talbot House, Toc representing T in the British Army's signals alphabet in the First World War. Talbot House was a rest and recreation centre for British soldiers in Belgium, established in 1915. It was named in honour of Gilbert Talbot, a soldier who had been killed earlier that year. The centre was established by his older brother, who was an Army chaplain. All soldiers were welcome there, regardless of rank. In 1920 a Christian youth centre called Toc H was established in London, and Toc H developed into an international, interdenominational organisation. An Australian branch was formed in Victoria in 1925. The "Four Points of the Toc H compass" were: 1. Friendship (To love widely), 2. Service (To build bravely), 3. Fairmindedness (To think fairly) and 4. The Kingdom of God (To witness humbly).

By himself in Australia, having deserted ship, and being in the country for the first time, Siegfried must have sought refuge at Toc H in Melbourne. He had just come from three months sailing on the *Gustav*, sailing from Ireland to Australia, and dodging icebergs. He must have felt grateful for having survived, for still being alive.

The other statements that beg explanation are the references to the "S.A." and the "Steel Helmet Organisation (Der Stahlhelm)". Siegfried seems to be quite forthcoming about his membership of these groups, as if it were something in his favour rather than the reverse. These references must relate to the period after he went back to Germany in 1931; he was too young to join these organisations beforehand.

What we must also take into account is the information he included in his application to appeal against his detention, which was made in December 1940. Despite the statements that Siegfried had made to the police in 1939-1940, in the application he asserts that there were no organisations in Germany with which he was connected: "Nil". So, it is an unresolved question.

In Australia, the only organisation to which he belonged was the Seamen's Union of Australia.

Figure 27: Hitler marching with S.S. officers

Der Stahlhelm was also called the League of Front-Line Soldiers. It was a First World War veteran's organisation existing from 1918 to 1935. During the last days of the Weimar Republic it was the paramilitary wing of the monarchist German National People's Party. For example, they operated as armed security guards at public meetings. After 1929 it took on an anti-republican and anti-democratic character. Its goals were a German dictatorship, the preparation of a revanchist program, and anti-parliamentarian action. It distinguished itself from the Nazi Party, and when Hitler came to power he worked to subordinate it. It was finally dissolved by decree of Adolf Hitler in November 1935.[3]

It is hard to see that Siegfried would have been a member of Der Stahlhelm. It was basically made up of old soldiers from World War I. When Siegfried went back to Germany, he was still only twenty. He only made the claim once, on 15 May 1940, when he went back to the police station in Sydney to tell them this information. The main point of saying it seemed to be that it was an organisation that was disbanded by Hitler when he came to power. He gave no evidence that he had been a member. Nor did he mention this at the internment inquiry hearing, and nor did Justice Simpson.

The other claim, which seems to have more foundation, is that he was a member of the S.A. There is a cryptic note in the files of the security forces from 25 April 1939, that says Siegfried "hands over his S.A. documents for safe custody". But then the note says they are "handed out again" (perhaps this means, at a later date).[4]

There are some claims in Siegfried's file that seem to be outlandish: he was a member of the German Secret Police; he was a member of the storm troopers in Berlin. It is likely that Siegfried had never even been to Berlin. He seems to have operated on an axis between Holzminden in the mid-west and Hamburg in the north.

However, the S.A. claim is backed by membership documents. And the S.A. is mentioned at the internment inquiry. Mr Norris (assisting the inquiry) says to Seigfried: "Then you went back to Germany in a German ship (in 1931)". "Yes. I joined the S.A. in Germany. I finally came back to Australia in August 1938 by the ship *Tisnaren*, from which I got a landing permit and took my discharge. I never handed over my S.A. documents to the German Consul in 1939. I showed them to the Consulate and that is all. I handed over no documents".[5]

Seigfried would have got a landing permit to come ashore while the ship was in port, but he did not take his discharge; he deserted. But the question here is what the business of the S.A. documents was about. What do we know about the S.A.?

S.A. stood for Sturmabteilung, or storm troopers. It was a paramilitary organisation associated with the Nazi Party. They wore brown shirts and ties, like Mussolini's Fascists. The SA was integral to the rise of Adolf Hitler and the Nazi Party, violently enforcing party norms and attempting to influence elections. They carried out attacks against Jews.

The SA was "purged" during the Night of the Long Knives in 1934 (30 June to 2 July), when the leader, Ernst Röhm, and around two hundred of the senior officers, were executed. Thereafter it lost most of its influence to the Schutzstaffel, or S.S. (the black-shirts), although the SA continued to exist until the end of the war.

Many of the stormtroopers believed in the socialist promise of National Socialism. They expected the Nazi regime to take more radical economic action, such as breaking up the vast landed estates of the aristocracy. In 1933, when Hitler took power in Germany, it had around two million members. The SA had its base among the unemployed and the working class.[6]

It is hard to interpret what Siegfried's membership of the SA meant, assuming it is true. As a member of the aristocracy, was he expressing rebellion against his family? Despite his brush with Toc H in 1928, was he amenable to the nationalistic cult of Hitler, bent on destroying the "Marxist enemy"?

Why would Seigfried be so open about being a member of the SA when it exemplified the values of the Nazi Party so closely? And why would he be so open with the Australian authorities whose task it was to root out people with Nazi sympathies? Seigfried's statement seems to be taken as uncontroversial, and it is simply brushed aside by Justice Simpson. Seigfried just says he was a member, and says nothing about how long he was a member, or what he did as a member.

There is also the puzzling statement, that he showed the SA documents to the German Consulate in 1939. One reason for this, however, would be that he was making sure he was eligible to receive the Reichstreue payments during the war. And perhaps this is the very reason for Seigfried's SA membership. The Wikipedia article quotes German historians of the 1930s who reported that many new SA members in the 1930s had come from left-wing youth groups. Perhaps Seigfried had been a member in name only, and was unaligned with the SA cause.

The example of another internee gives weight to this thesis. Wolf and Maria Klaphake migrated to Australia in 1935. He had a doctorate in chemistry, as well as excelling in physics and botany. In Australia he worked as a consultant chemist, and then for Industrial Microbiology, a company set up to fund his research and then exploit the inventions he made. Wolf and Maria left Germany because they did not like Nazism. They were not Jewish, but they were individualists and did not like Nazism's authoritarianism, its rigidity or its violence.

Klaphake had earned money from an invention in Germany, and he wanted to take this money with him to Australia. The price, ironically, was that he had to demonstrate his allegiance to Nazism by joining the Nazi Party. So, he came to Australia with a membership number. After the war was declared, the Australian authorities raided the German Consulate, and found the records of Nazi Party membership. Wolf Klaphake was listed.

It was enough to get him interned, despite his value to the Australian nation as a scientist. He arrived at Tatura at about the same time as Seigfried. We can assume that they met. Wolf's wife was also interned, and she arrived at Tatura at about the same time as Ellen Hottelmann. The tale of Klaphake and his wife is sad; she died before the end of the war. He was unable to obtain his release from the camp until the end of the war, and although he was then able to set up his own laboratory, he was unable to pursue the inventions that had interested him before the war.[7]

Figure 28: Wolf Klaphake

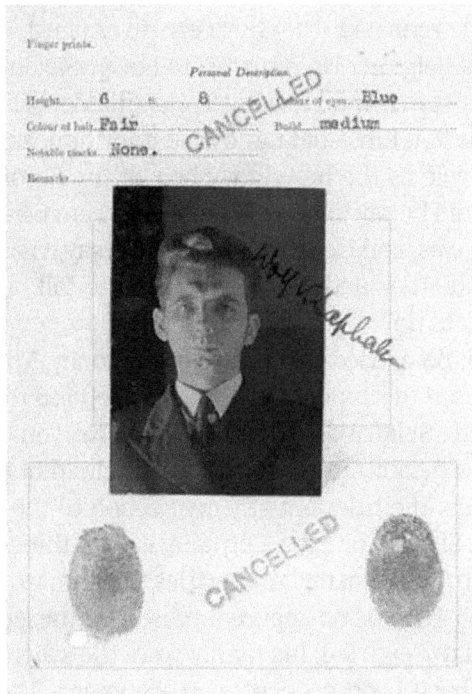

What seems likely is that Siegfried Hottelmann was a member of the SA in the same way that Klaphake was a member of the Nazi Party: not in reality, and only for the purpose of family survival, and to achieve escape from the Nazi regime. But in contrast to Seigfried, Wolf Klaphake did not accept the Reichstreue.

Klaphake's experience reminds us that internment was a gruelling trial. In a letter he wrote in 1944, Klaphake said, "I am not interested in eating, even if it is to the detriment of my physical well-being. All I do is to try to occupy my mind; to get interned is a way to get insane". Seigfried tended to be more upbeat, but that is not to say that his experience was not likewise gruelling.

However, I think there is more to Siegfried's membership of the SA than this. I don't think he was thinking of the future when he joined the SA. This might have been as early as 1932, and he did not leave Germany until 1936. What is more likely is that he joined the SA following an argument with his family (that is, his grandfather; and perhaps other relatives too, although none is ever mentioned).

Seigfried returned to Germany in August 1930 on the *Magdeburg*, via Belgium. He returned to Lower Saxony, and went to stay at Hanover rather than staying in Holzminden. His people (that is, people in the von Einsiedel family) sent for him, and wanted him to take up his role as the hereditary heir of the Baron title. But he refused. What did he say to them? Did he tell them what a wonderful place Australia was, and New Zealand? Did he say what he didn't like about his grandfather and the family? Did he talk about what he himself wanted to do?

But then, he needed to work to earn money. The grandfather must have refused to support him, and also refused to give him any work. He told Seigfried: "Go back where you came from". Presumably this meant Australia, as if to tell him that he would have to reject, not just the title, but any connection to the von Einsiedel lands in Lower Saxony, or even Germany itself. I think this is how to make sense of the statement, "Authorities told him to go back where you came from". There is no apparent reason for the local authorities to say this, and to Seigfried, his family were the salient authorities.

It must have been an explosive argument. The grandfather must have also threatened him, otherwise why would Seigfried be afraid of being exposed as a von Einsiedel? He was afraid after being exposed on the ship *Stassfurt* in Adelaide by the son of Siegfried's grandfather's gardener on the family estate in Lower Saxony. And the police at the interview on 26 July 1940 said he was "fidgety and went pale-looking when being questioned on the subject" (of the von Einsiedel name).

In need of work, Seigfried got a job as a sailor on a British ship, the *Adellen*, in March 1931. He went on a voyage to America and back. It gave him time to think about what he was going to do. I think that when Seigfried came back to Germany, he had found someone in the family who was sympathetic to him, and that was how he was able to go to the university at Rostock and study. He didn't say this to the police because it would have meant talking more about the von Einsiedel family. He simply said he worked as an interpreter for the next few years. It would have been plausible to the police, as none of them were bilingual, and Siegfried could speak both German and English fluently.

So, Siegfried was in Hamburg and Rostock, and he was angry with his family. This is sufficient explanation of why he joined the SA. It was not a strategic move, to ensure he would have an income in the internment camp: that would be looking too far ahead.

However, from Justice Simpson's perspective in 1946, the only relevance of admitting to membership of the SA (in May 1940) was so that you could claim the Reichstreue. This was an understandable reason.

15. The end of internment

An order revoking the detention orders for a specified list of ninety-one people was issued on 21 March 1946. The list includes Siegfried, Ellen and the two children. They were released on 4 April 1946.[1] The instructions accompanying the order note that "some family groups may have no home or shelter to go to, and it may be advisable, where the internees are agreeable, to release the head of the family first so that he could make suitable advance arrangements for the accommodation of his family.

"If this be done it would be desirable that the wife and children who remain behind for a few days should have the freedom of the camp if such be possible, as it is essential that the actual release orders be implemented as soon as possible…. In other words it would be most undesirable that any of these people should be turned out of the camp with nowhere to go and no means of subsistence".[2]

The camp was not empty yet. The internment inquiry resumed its deliberations in April 1946. By July, Justice Simpson had determined that 289 Germans should be deported, while 217 were released to reside in Australia.[3] The last family to leave Camp No. 3 was the Haering family in January 1948 (The daughter of the family remembered, "My parents always said that they had to lock the gates when they left").[4]

Figure 29: Siegfried, Ellen and two children, 1945

16. Life after release

Siegfried, Ellen and family stayed with Ellen's next-youngest sister Rose and her husband, Albert Stuart at 70 Bestic Street, Rockdale. Another baby was born, on 7 August 1946 — a son, Maximilian (Siegfried's father's name). It must have been crowded in the house. They stayed there for at least a couple of years before moving to their own place at Revesby, a small brick Housing Commission house.

Crowded it may have been, but this was not unusual in the post-war years. Housing was scarce and materials were scarce, so the building of new houses went slowly. Many families shared their houses with relatives. My own parents lived with my father's eldest brother and his family, probably for about four years until we found our own place. There was mum and dad and three of us children, one just born, the same as Siegfried and Ellen.

Figure 30: The Canberra

In the internment inquiry, Siegfried had talked about what he might do following the war. He had inventions and innovations in his mind, but the demands of family are pressing, and he returned to being a sailor.[1] Any ideas he might have had about returning to Germany were quashed. The reality of the devastation of the war in Europe began to be appreciated in Australia as soldiers began to come home. Siegfried must have had his own sources of information, as evidenced when he was interviewed by a reporter in Cairns in August 1946.

He was working as a sailor on a merchant ship, *Canberra*. The reporter asked about his title. Seigfried mentioned that a son had just been born (Maximilian, in early August 1946), "so the title will endure. But now it is a landless title, for the baronetcy of Einsiedel was among the lands of Saxony partitioned this year by Russia to settle her peasantry".[2]

Siegfried seemed to have made his decision to stay in Australia during the war, but this was not an added reason for it. Holzminden was not in East Germany; it was just to the west of the border, in West Germany (see Figure 36). So, we do not know what happened to the lands in Siegfried's absence.

Seigfried was realising that even though he had left the life of a Baron behind him, it still followed him around, as people knew about it and were curious. When his ship stopped at port, reporters would track him down and want to know about the title in Germany, what his life was like now, and what his reasons were for settling here. In Cairns, he talked about the Einsiedel family pledge "to live off the land. It was just 'not done' for the German nobility to set up industries on their estates", and the reporter even gives a physical description of him, "leaning on a ship rail near one of the giant cranes loading the ship".

Figure 31: Newspaper headlines in 1946

German Sailor Who Married Sydney Girl Is a Baron

MELBOURNE.—A slim Sydney dressmaker married a German sailor, Siegfried Hottelmann, against her father's wishes in July, 1939, and found, when she joined

DRESSMAKER WHO MARRIED GERMAN BARRON

MELBOURNE—A slim dressmaker married a German soldier, Ziefried Hottelmann, against her wishes in

Was A German Baron

A slim Sydney dressmaker married a German sailor, Siegfried Hottelmann, against her father's wishes in July, 1939, and found, when she joined him in internment in 1942, that he was really Freiherr Siegfried Emil Heinrich von Einsiedel, a German baron, whose title, dating beyond 1350, is probably one of the oldest in Europe.

The reporters listened when he talked about his interests: "He described his interest in experimenting with third dimensional films. He has a theory on which he has been working for six years".[3] He may not have had the means to pursue his interest, but he could talk about it, and people would listen.

The *Courier-Mail* in Brisbane reported that he had been a deck hand on the *Canberra* since his release from the internment camp five months ago, but he was "a 35-year-old German baron with 800 years of family tradition and estates in Saxony". Siegfried said "I am happy like this, because I am free. I would go home, but the Russians have seized my property. They would seize me, too".[4]

"A Special Reporter" from the *Daily Telegraph* in Sydney observed how he had first met Siegfried on the ship, and he had been painting on the boat deck. But "the same night he was entertaining a party of guests in the lounge of a Cairns hotel. He bowed and presented me with his card. It bore the name: Baron von Einsiedel and a seven-pointed coronet".[5]

Another piece appeared in a country newspaper in September 1946, untitled, simply as a human interest story:

Permit me to introduce you to Siegfried Hottelmann, able seaman on the well-known interstate vessel *Canberra*. A cultured and fluent conversationalist, and by no means dilletante scientist, who for six years has been working on the problem of three-dimensional films. He has toured New Zealand as an elephant driver with Wirth's Circus, taken the part of a German officer in the film 'Forty Thousand Horsemen', served under the mast in a German ship, came to Australia as a seaman on the *Tisnaren* after the war started, and, almost incredible as it may seem, was recognised by the ship's electrician as Freiherr Siegfried Emil von Einsiedel, a German Baron whose title goes back 700 years! And the electrician was the son of the Baron's head gardener! Security officers heard of the matter, and popped the Baron into a concentration camp! The Baron, it appears, early in 1939, had married a Sydney dressmaker under the assumed name of Siegfried Hottelmann, able seaman, much against the wishes of the girl's father, and she never learned her hubby's title till she and her babe joined him at Tatura (Vic) internment camp in 1942.

The story is strung together cheerfully. Mostly it is true, but some parts have been altered for the sake of smoothness. The *Tisnaren* arrived here in August 1938, not after the war had started, and Siegfried was not immediately "popped into a concentration camp" when his title became known to the authorities. (The *Tisnaren* was a casualty of war; it was sunk by an Italian submarine in May 1942 in the Atlantic, despite being a neutral ship. It was carrying Scotch whisky from England to South America.[6])

The article ends: "He has no time for Hitlerism, and he is happy in his home life out at Rockdale. Here, surely, is a story of drama and romance worthy any novelist's plan. To the ship's crew he is 'Baron' or 'Sig', as the fancy takes them".[7]

Figure 32: The house in Bestic Street, Rockdale

Siegfried seems to have been considering how he could combine the roles of seaman and baron in a way that was both practical and remunerative, interesting and open to opportunity. Perhaps this was an effect of his interview with Justice Simpson, Yet it was the work as a seaman that was most regular. There is no future evidence of his garnering a livelihood from his identity as a Baron.

84

Siegfried and Ellen must have discussed whether to recognise the title of Baron in their lives, and how. In January 1948, Siegfried went to the Registry of Births, Deaths and Marriages to make some changes to the entry for their marriage in 1939. A long note was handwritten into the record. It said that "In Column 3 (where his name is recorded), for 'Siegfried Emil Hottelmann' read 'Siegfried Emil Heinrich Freiherr von Einsiedel known as Hottelmann'".

Figure 33A: Marriage certificate, 1939

NEW SOUTH WALES

BIRTHS, DEATHS AND MARRIAGES REGISTRATION ACT 1995

REGISTRATION NUMBER
13886/1939

MARRIAGE CERTIFICATE

Date and place of marriage	Names and surnames of parties	Usual occupation	Usual place of residence
117	1st July 1939 Rockdale Municipality	Siegfried Emil Hottelmann	Salesman	3 Springfield Avenue Bexley Sydney N. Details
	Ellen Mary Royall	Dressmaker	134 Forest Road Arncliffe Sydney N. Details

Married at the District Registrar's Office, the King Edward Street Rockdale

The Consents of { } were given in writing to the Marriage of the Bridegroom.

The Consents of { } were given in writing to the Marriage of the Bride.

According to the rites of the Marriage Act 1899-1934

Conjugal status	Birthplace	Age	Father's name, mother's name and maiden surname	Father's occupation
Bachelor	Holzminden Germany	Years 28	Max Hottelmann (deceased) Ilse von Einsiedel (living)	Engineer
Spinster	Rockdale Sydney N. States	25	Herbert Augustus Royall Blanche Ellen Eaglestone	Clerk

This Marriage was solemnized between us { S. Hottelmann / E. M. Royall }

By me, E. Ediearne
Officiating Minister
District Registrar

In the presence of us { D. Royall / A. Silverwood }

RECEIVED and Registered by me, this 1st day of July 1939
E. Ediearne District Registrar.

Before accepting copies, sight unaltered original. The original has a coloured background.

REGISTRY OF BIRTHS DEATHS AND MARRIAGES

SYDNEY 11 September 2020

I hereby certify that this is a true copy of particulars recorded in a Register in the State of New South Wales, in the Commonwealth of Australia

Registrar

85

Figure 33B: Amendment to marriage certificate, 1948

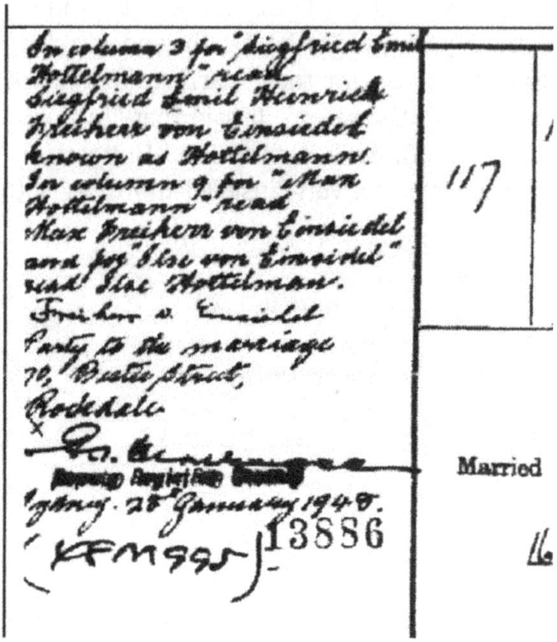

At this stage, Siegfried and Ellen were still living at 70 Bestic Street, Rockdale, with Rose and Albert. What did the annotation on the marriage record achieve? One assumes that it was a sign of their acceptance – both Siegfried and Ellen – that the title in Lower Saxony was a fact of their lives, regardless of its lack of practical implications. Given that their first child was named Sieglinde, perhaps it is no surprise that Siegfried's German's ancestry should be more openly acknowledged.

Siegfried and Ellen moved to their own house at Revesby sometime in the next few years, and they remained there until Siegfried's death in 1980. The three children grew up there and went to the local schools. Siegfried continued to work as a seaman. In 1949 he came to the attention of the security services again because he was working on a ship that had been chartered by the British Navy.

During the war the *Westralia* had served as an armed merchant cruiser, infantry landing ship and troopship, and after the war it had commenced a peacetime role in the Australian coastal passenger trade. But it was again requisitioned, this time under charter to the British Government, in August 1949, sailing to the

Mediterranean to transport troops. Although it was under naval orders, her crew consisted of Australian merchant seamen serving under Australian articles.[8]

Figure 34: The Westralia

The crew were scanned for security reasons. A memo was sent from the Deputy Director to the Director of the Commonwealth Investigation Service, marked "SECRET: Subject: Hottelmann and von Einsiedel". It noted:

> He is member of crew of *Westralia*, which left Sydney on 20 August 1949. As the *Westralia* is under charter to the Admiralty, the departure of this person is advised as a matter of interest.
>
> Hottelmann, who arrived in Aust on 28/8/1938, was interned on 2/8/1940 and released in 1946. Dossier 908 on the subject is held by the Directorate. There is no record of this person having applied for Naturalization. Naval authorities in this state have been advised of his departure. Signed R. Williams.[9]

The newspapers had expressed interest in the *Westralia* during August 1946: the fact that it was being repurposed from its peacetime work, the fact that it was being chartered by the British Navy, and the fact that it was to be a troop ship. The Director of the Commonwealth Investigation Service replied after a few days. The memo said, "von Einsiedel is married to an Australian woman and has two children. He was not considered to be a security risk by the

Commissioner (Mr Justice Simpson) in 1946. He was released unconditionally in Australia".[10]

And that, abruptly, is the end of the memo. It is clearly dismissive of the matter, as if to say, this has already been examined and been found absent of substance. (There were three children, not two, but the third was not born until after Siegfried and Ellen had been released from the internment camp.)

The *Westralia* returned to Australia on 1 March 1950 to be reconverted for peacetime service.[11]

17. Naturalisation

The Deputy Director's memo noted that there was no record of Siegfried having applied for naturalisation. And in fact, Siegfried did not get naturalised until 1966.[1] There is a conundrum here. Logically, it seems, there was no reason for him not to get naturalised. He was living in Australia, in a family, with three children who had all been born in Australia. He had decided to come here. He wasn't like some of the other people at Tatura, who discovered only after the war had ended that the homeland would not be bearable, or that the country they had come from no longer existed.

It must have seemed more and more obvious to him as time went on that he would never go back to Germany to live. Germany was not even a whole country anymore. It had been split into parts following the end of the war, and his own part of it, Lower Saxony, was in the U.S.S.R.: the Union of Soviet Socialist Republics. Perhaps that was the reason Siegfried did not get naturalised: he was holding onto a remnant, a memory of things that once were, and things that might have been, in a different world – if his parents had not died, if his grandfather had not been so difficult, if Hitler had not brought his sociopathic brand of brutal zeal, making everything madness.

Siegfried travelled overseas as a sailor. He went to Europe on the *Westralia*. He would have been well enough aware of world events. Did he ever desire to go back to Germany? When one has a family, there are two reasons to go back to your first home: to see it again for yourself, and to show it to your family. But if there are unhappy feelings about the place, you might wish to go by yourself, just to see. You might have demons you want to face, and it would be better not to drag the family into that.

If you were thinking about travelling overseas, you had to think about naturalisation. It would probably be safer to go overseas as a naturalised Australian. If there was trouble, you could go to the Australian embassy and be assured of help. There might even be some countries you could not go to unless you had an Australian passport. My conclusion is this: that Siegfried thought about travelling back to see his childhood homeland for years, and getting naturalised was, ironically, a necessary step in fulfilling that dream.

I don't think Siegfried had any qualms about getting naturalised. I think he was quite happy to be an Australian. As he said in 1946 to a reporter, "Australia to him was like the Land of the Sphinx for others: once you have been there, you always want to return". And he wasn't one of those who continually complain about their current situation and insist that "things were better back home". He accepted his lot. In the internment camp he looked to see what he could do to make the most of it.

So, I think Siegfried accepted naturalisation readily enough. It was probably difficult, and took such a long time, because it was like the last nail in the coffin of a German noble family that had roots almost a thousand years old. But it prepared the way for him to plan a visit back to Lower Saxony.

Perhaps as a mark that he accepted his position in Australian society, the following year he became a Justice of the Peace.[2] His name was Siegfried Emil Heinrich Hottelmann.

We know from the National Archives of Australia "Passenger Arrivals Index, 1898-1972" that Siegfried went overseas for one month in April-May 1972, by himself.[3] He flew back via Singapore. His second daughter, Ellen Waltraud, had come back from seventeen months working in England in August 1970.[4] Perhaps this foray by his daughter into the wider world emboldened him to make his own journey to see what time had done with his homeland.

I don't know where he went; the record does not say. But it is likely that he went to Germany, to Lower Saxony? These were the years of the Cold War, when Germany was split between East (for the Soviets) and West (for the Allies). Despite his comments to the journalist in Cairns in 1946, it is unlikely that he believed Holzminden was in East Germany and controlled by the USSR.

It was always possible to cross the borders during the Cold War, although it was difficult, and there were periodic interruptions and harassment of travellers. "Foreigners had to submit an itinerary to the East German state tourist office up to nine weeks in advance", and there were many other restrictions, including staying in state-owned 'Interhotels', where rooms cost five to ten times more than the price of the ordinary East German hotels.[5]

Figure 35: Passenger Arrival card for Siegfried Hottelmann

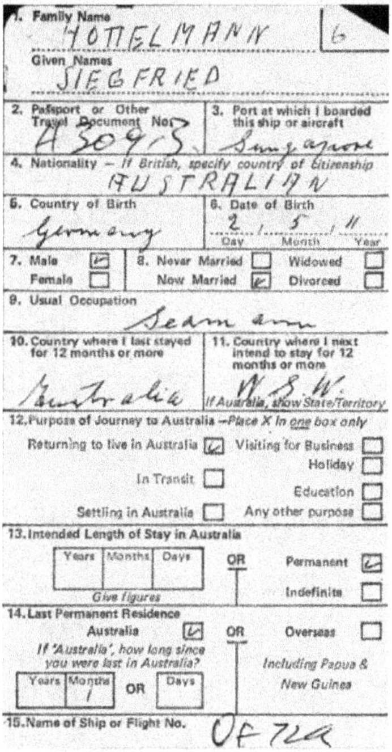
1. Family Name HOTTELMANN 6
Given Names SIEGFRIED
2. Passport or Other Travel Document No. A 509 / 3
3. Port at which I boarded this ship or aircraft Singapore
4. Nationality – If British, specify country of citizenship AUSTRALIAN
5. Country of Birth Germany
6. Date of Birth 2 / 5 / 11 (Day Month Year)
7. Male [x] Female [ ]
8. Never Married [ ] Now Married [x] Widowed [ ] Divorced [ ]
9. Usual Occupation Seaman
10. Country where I last stayed for 12 months or more Australia
11. Country where I next intend to stay for 12 months or more N.S.W. If Australia, show State/Territory
12. Purpose of Journey to Australia – *Place X in one box only*
Returning to live in Australia [x] Visiting for Business [ ]
Holiday [ ]
In Transit [ ]
Education [ ]
Settling in Australia [ ] Any other purpose [ ]
13. Intended Length of Stay in Australia
Years Months Days (*Give figures*) OR Permanent [x] Indefinite [ ]
14. Last Permanent Residence
Australia [x] OR Overseas [ ]
If 'Australia', how long since you were last in Australia?
Years Months 1 OR Days
Including Papua & New Guinea
15. Name of Ship or Flight No. QF 72A

It was only in 1972 that younger East Germans were permitted to travel to the West, so Siegfried went (we assume) at a time when social and political changes were underway.

A Welsh travel writer wrote this about travelling in East Germany: "Travelling from west to east through (the inner German border) was like entering a drab and disturbing dream, peopled by all the ogres of totalitarianism, a half-lit world of shabby resentments, where anything could be done to you. Your every step was dogged by watchful eyes".[6]

This was the atmosphere of the time, different to West Germany but still casting its shadow. As well as Holzminden, Siegfried would have wanted to visit Hamburg, where he had spent critical years as an adolescent, following the death of both of his parents. He had also been in Bremen, when embarking on his first sea voyage, and Rostock, where he had been to university. Fortunately, all of these places were in West Germany, in Lower Saxony, except Rostock (see Figure 36).

Whatever happened and whatever he thought about his brief travels, Siegfried did not travel outside Australia again.

Siegfried died on 28 December 1980 of lung cancer, aged sixty-nine. He was still living at Revesby with Ellen, where they had been resident for around thirty years. He was cremated at Rookwood Cemetery and his ashes were taken. His occupation according to his death certificate was "seaman".[7] It was the smallest indication of the vast scope of his life.

Ellen lived on until 14 July 2006. She died just before her ninety-third birthday.[8] She was cremated at Rookwood Cemetery and her ashes were taken. It was a long life for the "slim dressmaker who married a German Baron".

Figure 36: Holzminden in West Germany, 1983

18. Reflections and afterthoughts

Unlike many people we look for in our family history, there was a wealth of material available on Siegfried Hottelmann. Yet, we are still looking from a distance, and what we find are threads, not the whole garment. Siegfried's story is unusual and dramatic, but I was still left wondering about him. One of the questions was, did he know anything about Australia before he jumped on the sailing ship the *Gustav* in Ireland as a crew member in 1928?

Did Siegfried, as a child growing up in Germany, know anything about Australia before he went there? Germans had emigrated to Australia from various states of Germany since the early days of European settlement in Australia. Siegfried could have learned about Australia from stories told about any of these earlier ventures.

For example, in the period 1848 to 1854, about a thousand people emigrated from the Harz mountains in Lower Saxony to South Australia. Harz was a mining region, about 110 kilometres west of Holzminden, and the migrants were attracted to the copper mines north of Adelaide (as were Glenn Martin's ancestors on his father's side from the mines of Cornwall). Migration was encouraged by the local authorities in Harz, as the viability of the mines was waning. Stories of the migrants' success in the new colony were received warmly back home.[1]

There are many stories about individual German immigrants to Australia. Caroline Gaden tells the story of Doctor C.U.D. Schrader, who emigrated with his family from Schleswig-Holstein (north of Holzminden) to Walcha, New South Wales in 1853 and took up farming. The story is made more interesting because Doctor Schrader was a Baron.

The region he came from was fraught with tensions between Denmark and Germany, and at the time he emigrated, these tensions were spilling over. Doctor Schrader leant towards Germany; his father leant towards Denmark. Having emigrated, Doctor Schrader immersed himself in medicine and farming, without seeming to look back. He didn't seem to miss the aristocratic milieu in which he had grown up.[2]

Hahndorf in South Australia is acknowledged as Australia's oldest surviving German settlement. A director of the South Australian Company had visited London in 1838 to promote colonisation. There, he met a German pastor who was trying to help German Lutherans who were being persecuted by the King of Prussia. South Australia was suggested as an attractive place for the people to emigrate to, and financial support was also offered.[3]

In December 1838, the ship *Zebra* landed in Port Adelaide with 187 migrants, consisting of 38 families. The place they moved to was called Hahndorf because the ship's captain, Dirk Hahn, became involved in supporting their venture (dorf means village). Another 14 German families who had been living elsewhere in South Australia joined the group. Over the years the township grew and prospered, but it never lost track of its German origins.

In the Siegfried Hottelmann story, the German Lutheran women who were sent to South Australia in 1940 were the women who agitated to join their husbands at Tatura internment camp.

Other German families came to Australia in the nineteenth century with the same motivation as migrants from other countries: in search of land and a new start in life. In South Australia, many Germans moved to the Barossa Valley and established vineyards there. Many Germans also migrated to Queensland.

Whatever Siegfried knew about Australia as a child, it was enhanced by two years of living in Australia, from 1928 to 1930. From actual experience, Siegfried resolved that it was the place he would go to if he did not stay in Germany. Even 2-3 years in America (1936-1938) did not change this resolve.

The fact that Siegfried oscillated during the war between wanting to stay in Australia and wanting to go back to Germany showed that his mind was continually engaged with the issue. At one time he was prepared to take Ellen and the children with him and attune them to life with him as a Baron on the ancestral estates. But mostly, he was attracted to living in Australia after the war, despite the fact that it meant starting again from the beginning and reinventing himself.

I wonder what Siegfried felt about the reality of life after the war. He returned to the job of seaman, assuming no leadership positions, and consigning himself to a seaman's life. He could be away from home for weeks at a time, perhaps even months. I wonder what his life would have been like as a Baron, particularly in a family with such a long history. He would not have had the fragility of holding a recently invented title, but instead would have carried the history of an esteemed family. By extension he would have carried the history of a significant region of Germany, with a memory going back 800 years, and probably much longer.

In Switzerland there is a Benedictine abbey in the village of Einsiedeln. It is dedicated to Our Lady of the Hermits, in recognition of Meinrad of Einsiedeln, a hermit Catholic saint. He was born in 797 to an aristocratic German family. He became a priest, and it was reported that he performed miracles. His hermitage was established in 829. So, the roots of Siegfried's family would seem to run deep.[4]

Did Siegfried see his life as a failure, or as a liberation? Like the German colonists who had come to Australia in the nineteenth century, Siegfried may have seen the promise of Australia as the place for a new start. A humble situation may have been the pathway one takes in a new land, just like Doctor Schrader. Did Siegfried see himself as having been born just at the point of time in history when the Baronetcy failed, and the time of titles was vanishing? Did he have that young-man clarity about it?

The fact that his grandfather was insufferable could be seen simply as a symptom of the times. There were numerous times when Siegfried could have made his peace with his grandfather and accepted the role that his ancestry was offering him. But there never seems to be a time when he did so, or was even tempted to do so. And from the family's side, Siegfried never seems to have been given support. Among aristocratic families, regardless of country, there are many instances of young folk having their differences with their family, but still being provided for financially.

There may still be people alive who know the answers to some of these questions, but the answers are not available publicly. Siegfried held his own counsel. Beyond that brief period in 1946 when he let it be known that he was a Baron, and provided commentary to journalists on the matter, he subsequently lived his life as an ordinary seaman and a resident of suburban Revesby in Sydney.

There are questions too about the connections between Ellen Royall and my father. They were cousins. My father was born at Banksia, which is just north of Rockdale, and he grew up in the area. Ellen lived nearby at Arncliffe. They were born the same year. Did they know each other? Did they spend time with each other?

Figure 37: Family tree with Glenn Martin and Ellen Royall

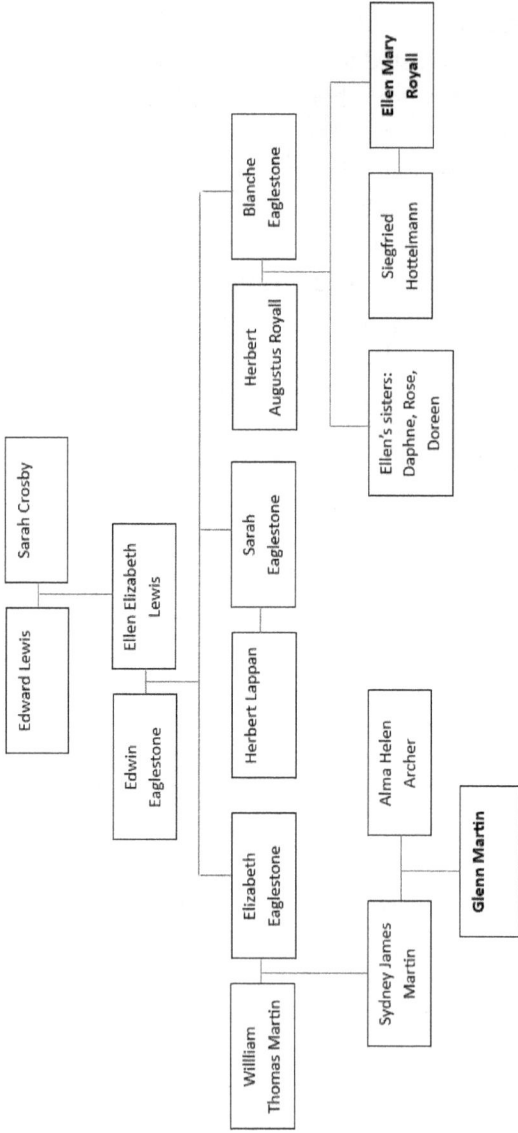

A pertinent story: when my siblings and I were young, our family went to Carss Park regularly to go swimming and have picnics on weekends during the summer. We looked forward to it. It was where we became proficient at swimming. It was a lovely place (as a child). I went back recently – it was over fifty years since I had been there – and it was still a lovely place.

I always assumed that we went there because it was the closest place from Greenacre to go swimming, that is, a safe place for young children. We did not have a car, and it was three bus trips (to Punchbowl, to Hurstville, then Carss Park), but we never found that daunting. It was the norm for our travel around Sydney. Later we went to Cronulla so that we could go to a surf beach.

Figure 38: Carrs Park in the 1920s

Now I think we went there because it reminded my father of when he was young. The same goes for my mother, too. She grew up at Marrickville, not far away. As far as I know, this was never said. I suppose, as children, we would not have listened anyway. We wanted to play and go swimming.

I am simply wondering. Both my parents are gone (my father died when I was sixteen). But it is an open question: did my father meet his cousins at Carrs Park when they were all young? In my story about Siegfried, Ellen's younger sister Doreen married Gordon Bowman, and they lived at Blakehurst. This is where Ellen went to stay when she was about to have her first baby. You could walk from the house to Carrs Park in five minutes.

And there is one more thing, a possible connection between my father and Ellen's sister Daphne, who married George Price. They lived in a house called "Rewa" in Taloombi Street, Gunnamatta Bay. Siegfried and Ellen had stayed with them for three or four days early in 1940. Consider the following memory.

When I was four, in July 1954, we stayed for six weeks in this street. We were about to move to 94 Cardigan Road Greenacre to live (mum and dad's own home finally), but apparently there was a period of time before it was available. We moved out of Uncle Norm's (my father's oldest brother) place at 96 Renown Avenue Punchbowl and stayed at Gunnamatta Bay. I didn't know why we went there. I knew it was a long way from dad's work (the Australian Gas Light Company at Mortlake) and from Greenacre or Punchbowl.

Mum and dad said it would be like a holiday. I think this is a strange thing to have happened. There is no explanation for it, but I remember it – mostly, the position of the house in relation to the water of Gunnamatta Bay, so I know it was in Taloombi Street. It could even be that we stayed with Daphne and George Price! I don't remember anything about people there. Perhaps they were away, and it was therefore convenient for us to stay in the house.

The more I think about this, the more likely it seems. This adds to the idea that my father had more to do with his family than I ever thought. So, he must have known about Ellen marrying the German in 1939. My father was already married (1935, to his first wife) and they had one child (born 1938).

I remember the time at Gunnamatta Bay because a few things in my early childhood stuck in my memory. I hated porridge, and one morning there was porridge left over and mum, I guess frustrated by my contrariness, gave me the saucepan and a spoon and told me to take it down to the sand on the bay and spoon it out. She said the seagulls will eat it. So, I remember we were staying in a house on the bay side of the street. I walked down the hillside to the sand through bush. I did not have to cross the road.

Family history is never finished. It is often illuminating, but it is even more often evocative. And ultimately, we are all connected.

As Siegfried said, "We are really the one and same race and belong together."

Figure 39: Plaque of Siegfried made in Tatura internment camp

Acknowledgments

My thanks to the National Archives of Australia for the extensive material on Siegfried Hottelmann.

My thanks also to the helpful staff at the Vaughan Evans Library at the Australian Maritime Museum.

The author

Glenn Martin lives in Sydney, although he lived in the bush at Kyogle on the far north coast of New South Wales for two decades. He has been a teacher at high schools and tertiary institutions, a manager of community services organisations, and a commentator on management, business ethics, employment law, and training and development. He has been the editor of publications for management and training professionals and an instructional designer for online learning. He is an independent scholar, a researcher and writer, and the author of over twenty books. His areas of interest include articulating reflections on experience, developing concepts about ethics and values, exploring family history, and (occasionally) writing poetry.

Glenn Martin's books

Stories/Reflections on experience

The Ten Thousand Things (2010)

Sustenance (2011)

To the Bush and Back to Business (2012)

The Big Story Falls Apart (2014)

The Quilt Approach: A Tasmanian Patchwork (2020)

Long Time Approaching (2023)

Travel with a Pen (2023)

Library Meets Book Fair (2024)

Books on ethics and values

Human Values and Ethics in the Workplace (2010)

The Little Book of Ethics: A Human Values Approach (2011)

The Concise Book of Ethics (2012)

A Foundation for Living Ethically (2020)

Future: The Spiritual Story of Humanity (2020)

Books on family history

A Modest Quest (2017)

The Search for Edward Lewis (2018)

They Went to Australia (2019)

No Gold in Melbourne: A Scottish Family in Australia (2021)

All the Rivers Come Together: Tracing Family (2022)

Poetry collections

Flames in the Open (2007)

Love and Armour (2007)

Volume 4: I in the Stream (2017)

Volume 3: That Was Then: The Early Poems Project (2019)

The Way Is Open (2020)

Local histories

Places in the Bush: A History of Kyogle Shire (1988)

The Kyogle Public School Centenary Book (1995)

Notes

1 Siegfried's place in my family and his own

[1] Meerovskii, B.V., 'Johann August Von Einsiedel', The Great Soviet Encyclopedia, The Free Dictionary, 1979, https://encyclopedia2.thefreedictionary.com/Johann+August+Von+Einsiedel accessed 15 March 2023.

[2] Panzer Paulus signed on the line, 26 September 1943, *The Sun* (Sydney), p. 1. Retrieved 24 January 2023, from http://nla.gov.au/nla.news-article231614020

[3] Germans on Soviet pay-roll, *Uralla Times* (NSW), 13 January 1949, p. 2. Retrieved 28 January 2023, from http://nla.gov.au/nla.news-article175343877

[4] Hottelmann, Emil Siegfried, Internees Inquiry by Mr Justice Simpson, National Archives of Australia (NAA), A367, C67918, p. 6.

[5] Date of birth of Siegfried Hottelmann: 2 May 1911 at Holzminden, Germany, Internee Service and Casualty Form for Siegfried Hottelmann, NAA, MP1103/2, PWN1355.

[6] Baron works as A.B. on steamer Canberra, *Cairns Post* (Queensland), 17 August 1946, p. 5, http://nla.gov.au/nla.news-article42506688 , accessed 10 January 2023.

[7] *Aliens Deportation Act 1946* (Cth), s. 3.

[8] NAA, A367, C67918, p. 6.

[9] Passenger list entry for Siegfried Hottelmann, *Dresden*, departing from Bremen, 17 December 1927 for Queenstown (Cork), Ireland, Bremen Passenger Lists, 1907-1939, Ancestry.com.

[10] Smith, Eugene W., *Trans-Atlantic Passenger Ships Past and Present*, George H. Dean Co., Boston MA, 1947, p. 79.

[11] Number of years as sailor is '10' for Siegfried Hottelmann, List or Manifest of Aliens Employed on the Vessel as Members of Crew, *Hagen*, departing Hamburg and arriving at Boston on 3 September 1936, US Arriving Passenger and Crew Lists, National Archives, Washington, accessed 11 January 2023.

[12] Gales and ice, *The Register* (Adelaide), 27 March 1928, p. 11.

2 Australia, the first time

[1] Gales and ice, *The Register*, 27 March 1928, p. 11; Barque Gustav arrives at Melbourne, *Daily Commercial News and Shipping List* (Sydney), 28 March 1928, p. 4.

[2] German barque to load wheat, *The Age*, 24 April 1928, p. 8.

[3] Seamen desert ship, *The Argus*, 14 April 1928, p. 31.

[4] NAA, A367, C67918, p. 71.

[5] German barque to load wheat, *The Age*, 24 April 1928, p. 8.

[6] Sinking of the collier Milora, The Argus (Melbourne), 9 March 1935, p. 23, http://nla.gov.au/nla.news-article12217493 retrieved 18 June 2024.

[7] NAA, A367, C67918, p. 6.

[8] NAA, A367, C67918, p. 8.

[9] Advertisement, *Auckland Star*, 21 March 1938, p. 16.

[10] St Leon, Mark, 'The circus in the context of Australia's regional, social and cultural history', *Journal of the Royal Australian Historical Society*, Vol. 72, Pt. 3, Dec 1986, pp. 204-25.

[11] 'People moving', *Australians 1888*, edited G. Davison, J.W. McCarty and A. McLeary, Fairfax, Syme & Weldon Associates, Broadway NSW, 1987, p. 241.

[12] Articles viewed on Papers Past (New Zealand): https://paperspast.natlib.govt.nz/ Articles: Untitled, *Poverty Bay Herald*, 10 October 1929, p. 4; Theatrical notes, *New Zealand Herald*, 17 November 1928, p. 8 (supplement).

[13] Advertisement, *Waimate Daily Advertiser*, 7 December 1929, p. 1.

[14] Elephants stampede, *Horowhenua Chronicle*, 15 January 1929, p. 5.

[15] This claim is unusual: elephants generally live 50-70 years in the wild and less in captivity; International Fund for Animal Welfare, https://www.ifaw.org/au/journal/elephant-faq, accessed 27 April 2024. However, there are instances of animals and birds living unusually long lives in captivity.

[16] *Auckland Star*, 10 March 1930, p. 10.

[17] *Poverty Bay Herald*, 26 February 1930, p. 4.

[18] Elephant's Mad Romp, *Otago Daily Times*, 13 May 1939, p. 3.

[19] Circus elephant mauls man, *Daily News* (Sydney), 12 March 1940, p. 3.

[20] Lost, an elephant, *Coffs Harbour Advocate*, 6 June 1939, p. 3.

[21] *Auckland Star*, 21 March, 1930, p. 8.

[22] Ulimaroa stowaway, *The Sun* (Sydney), 29 July 1930, p. 9.

[23] Stowaways on Ulimaroa, *The Argus* (Melbourne), 4 October 1930, p. 19.

[24] Collated from Shipping Intelligence, *The Age* (Melbourne); Maritime News, *Daily Standard* (Brisbane); Overseas Vessels in Port, *Sydney Morning Herald* (Sydney); Harbor Removals, *Daily Telegraph* (Sydney);

Shipping, *The West Australian* (Perth); Shipping Intelligence, *The Brisbane Courier*; Shipping Movements, *The Advertiser* (Adelaide).

3 Return to Germany

[1] NAA, A367, C67918, p. 72.
[2] *Adellen*, Scottish Built Ships, https://www.clydeships.co.uk/
[3] Shipping Intelligence, *Western Daily Press* (Yeovil, England), 3 May 1932; Shipping News, *Hull Daily Mail* (Hull, England), 4 July 1932.
[4] *Adellen*, U-boat.net, https://uboat.net/allies/merchants/ship/1363.html
[5] NAA, A367, C67918, p. 72.
[6] Private communication, Ellen Waltraud Hottelmann to Glenn Martin, 14 Oct 2023.
[7] Hottelmann, Siegfried Emil, Tatura Internment Camp, National Security (Aliens Control) Regulations, Application For Leave To Submit Objections Against Detention Order, NAA, MP529/8.
[8] Letter from Collector of Customs, South Australia to The Secretary, Department of the Interior, Canberra, Title: 'Siegfried E. Hottelmann, German deserter from M.S. "Tisnaren" at Port Adelaide on 11.9.1938', Siegfried E HOTTELMANN deserter – passport, p. 12, National Archives of Australia, D596, 1938/5650.
[9] List or Manifest of Aliens Employed on the Vessel as Members of Crew, *Hagen.*
[10] Count punches clock for Ford, *Oshkosh Daily Northwestern*, 31 May 1930, Oshkosh, Wisconsin, p. 4.
[11] Baron works as A.B. on steamer Canberra, *Cairns Post.*

4 Exploring America, returning to Australia

[1] Hottelmann, NAA, MP529/8.
[2] *Tisnaren* arrived in Melbourne with cargo of timber from Vancouver, 'At sea and in port', *Age*, 29 August 1938, p. 8, http://nla.gov.au/nla.news-article166712505 accessed 7 February 2023.
[3] *M.V. Tisnaren* to leave San Francisco after Vancouver, 'Shipping, Mails and Markets', *Newcastle Sun*, 1 June 1938, p. 2, accessed 15 March 2023.
[4] Joined crew one and half months ago, Particulars required if any members of colored crew of a vessel are missing at final muster (NB 'colored crew' includes aliens), National Archives of Australia, D596, 1938/5650, p. 15.
[5] Untitled, *Wingham Chronicle and Manning River Observer*, 13 September 1946, p. 1.

[6] Shipping reports, *Daily Commercial News and Shipping List* (Sydney): 25 August, 26 August, 3 September 1938.

[7] 'Vessels inward and outward bound to and from Australasian ports', *Daily Commercial News and Shipping List* (Sydney), 9 September 1938, p. 8, http://nla.gov.au/nla.news-article162058939, accessed 22 March 2023.

[8] Untitled, *Chronicle* (Adelaide), 15 September 1938, p. 47.

[9] Advertisement, *Daily Commercial News and Shipping List* (Sydney), 21 December 1934, p. 1.

[10] Date of departure from Adelaide, Letter from Collector of Customs, SA to The Secretary, Department of the Interior, Canberra, National Archives of Australia, D596, 1938/5650, p. 12; *Tisnaren* contract to convey sugar from Queensland to London, 'Sugar vessels', *Daily Commercial News and Shipping List* (Sydney), 17 September 1938, p. 3.

[11] Particulars required if any members of colored crew of a vessel are missing at final muster, National Archives of Australia, D596, 1938/5650, p. 15.

[12] Siegfried Emil Hottelmann, 'Prohibited Immigrant', South Australia Police Gazette, 21 September 1938, p. 372.

[13] German sailor who married Sydney girl Is a baron, *News* (Adelaide), 2 February 1946, p. 1; Dressmaker who married German Barron[sic], *Barrier Miner* (Broken Hill), 2 February 1946, p. 4.

[14] All German Merchantmen Ordered Home; Four In Australian Waters, *Border Watch* (Mount Gambier), 29 September 1938, p. 1.

[15] Can See People Smiling Again: Jewish Immigrant Is Happy, *Recorder* (Adelaide), 16 September 1938, p. 2.

[16] Particulars required if any members of colored crew of a vessel are missing at final muster (NB 'colored crew' includes aliens), NAA, D596, 1938/5650, p. 15.

[17] Siegfried E. Hottelmann deserter – passport, NAA, D596, 1938/5650, pp. 12-16.

[18] Police Gazette, South Australia. 21 Sep 1938.

[19] Swedish seaman jailed, deportation order sought, *Daily News* (Perth), 2 February 1935, p. 16.

[20] Memorandum from Immigration & Passports Office, Melbourne to Secretary, Department of the Interior, Canberra re Siegfried's work on dredge, NAA, D596, 1938/5650, p. 11; NAA, D596, 1938/5650, Letter from F. Terry, Collector of Customs, South Australia to Siegfried Hottelmann re passport, dated 29 March 1939, p. 4.

[21] Memorandum from Immigration & Passports Office, Melbourne to Secretary, Department of the Interior, Canberra, dated 30 December 1938, NAA, D596, 1938/5650, p. 11; *Mungana* laid up, 'N.Z. & interstate vessels in port at Sydney', *Daily Commercial News and Shipping List* (Sydney), 28

December 1938, p. 8, http://nla.gov.au/nla.news-article162049810, accessed 7 February 2023.

[22] Memorandum from Immigration & Passports Office, Melbourne to Secretary, Department of the Interior, Canberra, dated 30 December 1938, NAA: D596, 1938/5650, p. 11.

[23] Australian Museums and Galleries: https://aumuseums.com/sa/yorke-and-lower-north/carn-brae and https://carnbraeportpirie.com.au/

[24] Collated from shipping items in Australian newspapers.

[25] Dates of the ship's movements come from daily shipping reports in numerous Australian newspapers.

5 Approval to stay in Australia

[1] Memos between Collector of Customs SA and Sub-Collector of Customs, Port Pirie, NAA, D596, 1938/5650, pp. 5-8.

[2] Letter from F. Terry, Collector of Customs, South Australia to Siegfried Hottelmann, dated 29 March 1939, NAA, D596, 1938/5650, p. 4.

[3] Migrant landing restrictions, *The Herald* (Melbourne), 7 February 1939, p. 10.

[4] Memos between Collector of Customs SA and Sub-Collector of Customs, Port Pirie, NAA, D596, 1938/5650, pp. 1-2.

[5] Trove: dates of performances of Wirth's Circus in various newspapers, 1938-1940; 'The Circus', *Smith's Weekly* (Sydney), 1 April 1939, p. 19, http://nla.gov.au/nla.news-article234595796 , accessed 23 March 2023.

[6] The circus, *Smith's Weekly*, (Sydney), 1 April 1939, p. 19.

[7] Sydney Trocadero, Wikipedia, https://en.wikipedia.org/wiki/Sydney_Trocadero Retrieved 22 March 2024.

[8] Advertising, *Daily Telegraph*, 5 April 1939, p. 22; *Daily Telegraph*, 20 May 1939, p. 4.

[9] Evidence by Ellen Hottelmann, Internees Inquiry, NAA, A367, C67918, p. 7.

[10] Divorce Papers, Herbert Augustus Royall and Blanche Ellen Royall, divorced 6 November 1921, New South Wales State Archives & Records, 786/1918. Marriage certificate of Herbert Augustus Royall and Gladys Alma Hector, married 1925 at Hurstville, Registry of Births, Deaths and Marriages, New South Wales, 2598/1925.

[11] Marriage certificate of Siegfried Emil Hottelmann and Ellen Mary Royall, married 1 July 1939 at Rockdale, Registry of Births, Deaths and Marriages, New South Wales, 13886/1939. Note 1: the index has six entries for the marriage, but all relate to 13886/1939; Note 2: the

certificate I purchased on 24/10/2016 includes a handwritten amendment to Siegfried's name to include "von Einsiedel" as part of his name.

[12] German sailor who married Sydney girl is a baron, *News* (Adelaide), 2 February 1946, p.1.

[13] Hottelmann, Emil Siegfried, Schedule 1, Internees Inquiry, NAA, A367, C67918, p. 5.

[14] Death of Peter Royall, 1899, Registry of Births, Deaths and Marriages, 3048/1899.

[15] Marriage of Thomas Silverwood to Annie Croake/Kearns at Redfern, 1939, Registry of Births, Deaths and Marriages, 1133/1939.

[16] NAA, A367, C67918, p. 9.

[17] NAA, A367, C67918, p. 6.

[18] NAA, A367, C67918, p. 8. Notes: The document states "Masson", but there is no such ship in the shipping reports in 1939, and there is a ship called *Macedon*, for which the agent was Howard Smith.

6 September 1939: war is declared

[1] "Wanderer", Busy street and quiet corner: Transport assembly, *Recorder* (Port Pirie, SA), 2 September 1939, p. 2.

[2] *News* (Adelaide), 2 February 1946, p. 1; *Barrier Miner* (Broken Hill), 2 February 1946, p. 4.

[3] 'Forty Thousand Horsemen', Wikipedia, https://en.wikipedia.org/wiki/Forty_Thousand_Horsemen , accessed 14 February 2023.

[4] Credits for film, 'Forty Thousand Horsemen', BFI, https://www2.bfi.org.uk/films-tv-people/4ce2b6aa82676 , accessed 14 February 2023.

[5] NAA, A367, C67918, p. 82.

[6] 'Forty Thousand Horsemen', Wikipedia, https://en.wikipedia.org/wiki/Forty_Thousand_Horsemen

[7] Hottelmann, Siegfried Emiel Heinrich, also known as Baron von Einsiedel, NAA, SP11/2, p. 3, accessed 30 March 2023.

[8] NAA, A367, C67918, pp. 76, 79.

[9] NAA, A367, C67918, p. 9.

[10] Caledonian Maritime Research Trust, https://www.clydeships.co.uk/ accessed 2 May 2024.

[11] NAA, A367, C67918, p. 62.

[12] NAA, A367, C67918, p. 90.

[13] NAA, A367, C67918, p. 76.

[14] NAA, A367, C67918, p. 82.

[15] NAA, A367, C67918, p. 76.

[16] NAA, A367, C67918, p. 68.
[17] NAA, A367, C67918, p. 78.
[18] NAA, A367, C67918, p. 75.
[19] NAA, A367, C67918, p. 59.
[20] Hottelmann, Ellen Mary, NAA, SP11/2, p. 3, accessed 30 March 2023.
[21] NAA, A367, C67918, pp. 100-103.
[22] NAA, A367, C67918, p. 61.
[23] Internee/Prisoner of War Service and Casualty Form: Sieglinde Ellen Hottelmann, NAA, MP1103/1, NF1650.
[24] NAA, A367, C67918, p. 59.
[25] NAA, A367, C67918, p. 57.

7 Siegried is interned

[1] NAA, A367, C67918, pp. 55-56.
[2] NAA, MP1103/2, PWN1355.
[3] Knee, Lurline & Arthur, *Marched In*, published by Lurline & Arthur Knee for the Tatura & District Historical Society, 2008, p. 7-8.

9 Siegfried at Tatura

[1] NAA, A367, C67918, p. 10.
[2] Hottelmann, NAA, MP529/8.
[3] NAA, A367, C67918, p. 10.
[4] NAA, A367, C67918, p. 119.
[5] NAA, A367, C67918, p. 53.
[6] Ellen Mary Hottelmann, Internee/Prisoner of War Service and Casualty Form, NAA, MP1103/1, NF1649.
[7] Purposely sought internment, 28 Feb 1946, *Advocate* (Burnie, Tasmania), p. 5. Retrieved February 20, 2024, from http://nla.gov.au/nla.news-article68964634
[8] NAA, A367, C67918, p. 7.

10 Ellen joins Siegfried in internment

[1] NAA, A367, C67918, p. 132.
[2] Nobility Titles: https://nobilitytitles.net/german-nobility-ranks/ Accessed 30 January 2023.
[3] NAA, A367, C67918, p. 119.
[4] NAA, A367, C67918, p. 32.
[5] NAA, A367, C67918, p. 32.
[6] Monteath, Peter, *Captured Lives: Australia's wartime internment camps*, NLA Publishing, Canberra, 2018, p. 166

[7] NAA, A367, C67918, p. 11.
[8] Knee & Knee, *Marched In*, p. 132.
[9] Author of *Who Gets Believed?*, Harvill Seeker, London, 2023, p. 158.
[10] NAA, A367, C67918, pp. 46-48.
[11] NAA, A367, C67918, pp. 28-29.
[12] NAA, A367, C67918, pp. 19-24, 39-44.
[13] NAA, A367, C67918, pp. 27, 45.
[14] NAA, A367, C67918, p. 18.
[15] NAA, A367, C67918, pp. 105-107.

11 Associates in the camp

[1] NAA, A367, C67918, pp. 105-107.
[2] Frederick [Fritz] Theodore Picker [Application for Naturalisation] and Marianne Picker [Both Interned], NAA, ST1233/1, N27964 PART 1, p. 67.
[3] And so they sang the Nazi song, *Daily Telegraph*, 2 May 1934, p. 4. Retrieved 9 March 2024 from http://nla.gov.au/nla.news-article246435973
[4] This is Australia's Nazi No. 2, *Truth*, 5 January 1936, p. 13. Retrieved 9 March 1924 from http://nla.gov.au/nla.news-article169590593
[5] Nazi hambone purveyor, *Daily News*, 5 December 1938, p. 2. Retrieved 9 March 1924 from http://nla.gov.au/nla.news-article236317488
[6] Women fined for demonstration, *Daily Telegraph*, 8 February 1939, p. 9. Retrieved 9 March 2024 from http://nla.gov.au/nla.news-article247450228
[7] Stone thrown through window, *Sydney Morning Herald*, 4 September 1939, p. 9. Retrieved 9 March 1924 from http://nla.gov.au/nla.news-article17619899
[8] Sydney action: internment of aliens, *Kalgoorlie Miner* (WA), 5 September 1939, p. 4. Retrieved 9 March 2024 from http://nla.gov.au/nla.news-article94848611

12 Considering post-war life

[1] NAA, A367, C67918, p. 114.
[2] Family group: Hottelmann and Dannenberg families, photo by Ronald Leslie Stewart, Tatura, 10 March 1945, Australian War Memorial collection C327726, accession number 030244/10.
[3] NAA, A367, C67918, p. 11.
[4] NAA, A367, C67918, p. 132.
[5] NAA, A367, C67918, p. 126.

13 Release from internment

[1] Knee & Knee, *Marched In*, p. 147.

[2] NAA, A367, C67918, p. 5.

[3] The following passage on the interviews with Justice Simpson is drawn from NAA, A367, C67918, p. 4-11.

[4] Gladys Alma Royall, Death Notices, *Sydney Morning Herald,* 22 February 1944.

[5] Herbert Augustus Royall, died 30 June 1945, death certificate, New South Wales Registry of Births, Deaths and Marriages, 17478/1945.

[6] George Ernest Royall, died 1942, Registry of Births, Deaths and Marriages, Victoria, 2712/1942.

[7] Blanche Ellen Royall, died 23 June 1950, death certificate, New South Wales Registry of Births, Deaths and Marriages, 007557/1950.

[8] For example: German Sailor Who Married Sydney Girl Is a Baron, *News* (Adelaide), 2 February 1946, p. 1. Retrieved January 10, 2023, from http://nla.gov.au/nla.news-article128344645

[8] Hottelmann, NAA, MP529/8, p. 3.

14 Siegfried's involvement in organisations

[1] German Boy Scouts / Pfadfinderen, https://histclo.com/youth/youth/org/sco/country/ger/scoutger.htm ; Wandervogel, https://en.wikipedia.org/wiki/Wandervogel accessed 13 March 2024.

[2] NAA, A367, C67918, p. 9.

[3] Der Stahlhelm, Bund der Frontsoldaten, Wikipedia, https://en.wikipedia.org/wiki/Der_Stahlhelm,_Bund_der_Frontsoldaten Retrieved 8 March 2024.

[4] NAA, A367, C67918, p. 50.

[5] NAA, A367, C67918, p. 8.

[6] S.A.: Sturmabteilung, Wikipedia, https://en.wikipedia.org/wiki/Sturmabteilung Retrieved 14 March 2024.

[7] German intern: Wolf Klaphake, http://uncommonlives.naa.gov.au/timeline.asp?lID=1 Retrieved 10 February 2023; note, this web page is no longer available (14 February 2024). See also, NAA: MP529/8, Klaphake, W.

15 The end of internment

[1] Siegfried Emil Hottelmann, Internee/Prisoner of War Service and Casualty Form, NAA, MP1103-1, PWN13660

[2] NAA, A367, C67918, p. 4.
[3] Delay in alien deportation: Bill to extend powers, *The Age*, 27 July 1946. Retrieved 10 January 2023, from http://nla.gov.au/nla.news-article206368806
[4] Knee & Knee, *Marched In*, p. 146.

16 Life after release

[1] *Cairns Post*, 17 August 1946, p. 5; Siegfried Emil Heinrich Hottelmann address, 1 Cuthbert St Revesby: 1968, 1972, 1977, 1980, Australia, Electoral Rolls, 1903-1980, Ancestry.com, accessed 3 February 2023.
[2] Baron works as A.B. on steamer *Canberra, Cairns Post*.
[3] *Cairns Post*, 17 August 1946.
[4] Baron sails as deck hand, *Courier-Mail*, 25 August 1946, p. 7. Retrieved 10 January 2023, from http://nla.gov.au/nla.news-article49335579
[5] Sailor has name for his social activities, *Daily Telegraph*, 27 August 1946, p. 9. Retrieved January 10, 2023, from http://nla.gov.au/nla.news-article248532236
[6] *Tisnaren*, War Sailors, https://warsailors.com/forum/archive/forum/read.php-1,10659,18399.html Retrieved 17 March 2024.
[7] Untitled, *Wingham Chronicle and Manning River Observer*, 13 September 1946, p. 1. Retrieved, 20 April 2023 from https://newspaperarchive.com/wingham-chronicle-and-manning-river-observer-sep-13-1946-p-1/
[8] "Secret Mission" For Westralia, *Newcastle Sun* (NSW), 17 Aug 1949, p. 1. Retrieved March 2, 2024, from http://nla.gov.au/nla.news-article158284709
[9] NAA, A367, C67918, p. 135.
[10] NAA, A367, C67918, p. 134.
[11] Laxon, W.A., *Huddart Parker: A Famous Australasian Shipping Company, 1876-1961*, Nautical Association of Australia, Melbourne, 2008, p. 197.

17 Naturalisation

[1] Siegfried Emil Heinrich Hottelmann, Certificate of Naturalization, Government Gazette Notices, Commonwealth of Australia Gazette, 3 February 1966, p. 455.
[2] Appointments, Commission of the Peace for the State of New South Wales, Government Gazette, Issue No. 87, 11 August 1967, p. 2909.

[3] Siegfried Hottelmann, Passenger Arrivals Records, 24 May 1972, National Archives of Australia, A1197, 9788232, pp. 589-590.
[4] Ellen Waltraud Hottelmann, Passenger Arrivals Records, 29 August 1970, National Archives of Australia, A1197, 12206346, pp. 987-988.
[5] Crossing the inner German border during the Cold War, Wikipedia, retrieved from https://en.wikipedia.org/wiki/Crossing_the_inner_German_border_duri ng_the_Cold_War on 3 March 2024.
[6] Morris, Jan, *Fifty years of Europe: an album*, Villard, New York, 1997, p. 71.
[7] Death certificate of Siegfried Emil Hottelmann, died 28 December 1980; usual residence: 1 Cuthbert St Revesby; place of birth: Holzminden, Germany; children: Sieglinde 40 years, Ellen 35, Maximillian 34; New South Wales Registry of Births, Deaths and Marriages, 233/1981.
[8] Death notice of Ellen Hottelmann, died 14 July 2006, *Sydney Morning Herald*, 17 July 2006.

18 Reflections and afterthoughts

[1] Meiss, Corinna, Gluckauf: Emigration Desirable, *Traces*, 21st edition, 2022, pp. 14-16.
[2] Gaden, Caroline, *From Baron to Battler*, 2012, ebook, https://www.smashwords.com/books/view/129058
[3] History of Hahndorf, https://hahndorfsa.org.au/history/
[4] Einsiedeln Abbey, Wikipedia, https://en.wikipedia.org/wiki/Einsiedeln_Abbey

Sources for the images

Figure 1: The Dresden p. 2

SSMaritime website. Note: the 'Ormuz' was renamed in 1927 to become the 'Dresden'. http://ssmaritime.com/Ormuz-1921-27.htm accessed 1 May 2024.

Figure 2: The Gustav p. 3

The 'Austrasia' after being renamed 'Gustav', photograph, PRG 1373/12/25, A.D. Edwardes Collection, State Library, South Australia.

Figure 3: Elephant handler feeding the elephants, Wirth's Circus, 1930s p. 5

Feeding the elephants, circa 1932, Wirth's Circus, photograph by Sam Hood, Mitchell Library, State Library of New South Wales.

Figure 4: The Magdeburg p. 8

Magdeburg, cargo ship, built 1925, Ship Spotting, https://www.shipspotting.com/photos/1566548 accessed 29 April 2024.

Figure 5: The Adellen p. 10

Scottish-Built Ships. Adellen: completed 9/1930. 4,735 tons, 460 ft long. Built by Blythswood Shipbuilding Co Ltd, Glasgow. First owner: Adellen Shipping Co. Ltd., London - Bernuth, Lembcke & Co., New York. Fate: torpedoed 22/2/1942. https://www.clydeships.co.uk accessed 24 April 2024.

Figure 6: Count von Einsiedel in America, 1930 p. 12

Count punches clock for Ford, *Oshkosh Daily Northwestern*, 31 May 1930, Oshkosh, Wisconsin, p 4.

Figure 7: The Tisnaren p. 14

Ships Nostalgia, Tisnaren, general cargo ship, https://www.shipsnostalgia.com/media/tisnaren.345325 accessed 17 March 2024.

Figure 8: Carn Brae at 32 Florence Street, Port Pirie p. 18

Photo by author.

Figure 9: Advertisement for Wirth's Circus, 1930s p. 21

Wirth's Circus Advertisement, 1930s, object no. 2012/104/39, Powerhouse collection, Sydney.

Figure 10: The Sydney Trocadero, 1930s p. 23

Radio station 2CH's Children's Christmas party at the Trocadero Ballroom in Sydney, 22 December 1936, photograph by Sam Hood, Mitchell Library, State Library of New South Wales.

Figure 11: Boarding house at 134 Forest Road, Arncliffe p. 24

Photo by author.

Figure 12: Poster for the movie, "Forty Thousand Horsemen" p. 28

IMDb, https://www.imdb.com/title/tt0033307/mediaviewer/rm2816301568 accessed 13 March 2023.

Figure 13: Siegfried Hottelmann, photo from police file p. 29

Hottelmann, Siegfried Emiel Heinrich, also known as Baron von Einsiedel, National Archives of Australia, SP11/2, p. 3.

Figure 14: The William Macarthur p. 31

Website: Scottish Built Ships, www.clydeships.co.uk accessed 7 May 2024.

Figure 15: Ellen Royall, from police file p. 35

Hottelmann, Ellen Mary, National Archives of Australia, SP11/2, p. 4.

Figure 16: Kenton Court in Cathedral Street, Woolloomooloo p. 38

Photo by author.

Figure 17: Tatura Camp 1, 1943, showing division between compounds A and B p. 43

Photograph by James Tait, Australian War Memorial, accession no, 052408.

Figure 18: Tatura Camp 1 p. 44

Tatura Camp 1, viewed from the Garrison Quarters, *Marched In: Seven Internment and Prisoner of War Camps in the Tatura Area*, Lurline and Arthur Knee, published by Lurline and Arthur Knee, 2008, p. 21.

Figure 19: Tatura Camp 3; woodcuts of the camp, by Ludwig Hirschfeld-Mack p. 45

German-Australian website: http://www.germanaustralia.com/e/tatura.htm accessed 10 January 2023.

Figure 20: Knitted items for Tatura internees' enterprise p. 51

Photographs of knitted items from Siegfried Hottelmann at Tatura and District Historical Society museum, donated by Sieglinde Hottelmann.

Figure 21: Johannes Frerck p. 55

Photo on passport of Johannes Frerck, NAA, C415, 1 (Part 2), p. 3.

Figure 22: Hottelmann family photo with Dannenbergs p. 59

Family group: Hottelmann and Dannenberg families, Tatura, 10 March 1945, photo by Ronald Leslie Stewart, Australian War Memorial, Collection C327726, accession number 030244/10.

Figure 23: Sketch of Tatura Camp 3 by C. Gluckner p. 61

Tatura Camp 3, Family Barracks, sketch by C. Gluckner, 1942, *Marched In: Seven Internment and Prisoner of War Camps in the Tatura Area*, Lurline and Arthur Knee, published by Lurline and Arthur Knee, 2008, p. 64.

Figure 24: Justice William Simpson p. 64

William Ballantyne Simpson (1894–1966), photograph 1942, Australian Dictionary of Biography, https://adb.anu.edu.au/biography/simpson-william-ballantyne-11700 accessed 29 April 2024.

Figure 25: Map of Germany p. 66

States of the Federal Republic of Germany, Nations Online Project, https://www.nationsonline.org/oneworld/countries_germany.htm accessed 15 March 2023.

Figure 26: Australian Sea Scouts in 1930s p. 71

Sea Scouts, 1932, Kogarah Bay, Kogarah Historical Society, accessed 28 April 2024.

Figure 27: Hitler marching with S.S. officers p. 73

SS: History, Meaning, & Facts, Britannica, https://www.britannica.com/topic/SS accessed 29 April 2024.

Figure 28: Wolf Klaphake p. 76

Dr Wolf Klaphake, Internment Camp Registration Card, NAA, D1901, K1056, p.13.

Figure 29: Siegfried, Ellen and two children, 1945 p. 79

Hottelmann family, Tatura, March 1945, Victorian Collections, https://victoriancollections.net.au/items/63d5e8124368f1bc5ec100 d9 accessed 17 March 2024.

Figure 30: The Canberra p. 80

S.S. Canberra was a passenger vessel with a capacity for 410 passengers, managed by Howard Smith. It was sold off to a Greek company in late 1947. Caledonian Maritime Research Trust, www.clydeships.co.uk accessed 2 May 2024.

Figure 31: Newspaper headlines in 1946 p. 81

German sailor who married Sydney girl is a Baron, *News* (Adelaide), 2 February 1946, p. 1; Dressmaker who married German Baron, *Barrier Miner* (Broken Hill), 2 February 1946, p. 4; Was a German Baron, *Northern Advocate* (New Zealand), 4 May 1946, Page 7.

Figure 32: The house in Bestic Street, Rockdale p. 83

Photo by author.

Figure 33A: Marriage certificate, 1939 p. 84

Marriage certificate of Siegfried Emil Hottelmann and Ellen Mary Royall, married 1 July 1939 at Rockdale, Registry of Births, Deaths and Marriages, New South Wales, 13886/1939.

Figure 33B: Amendment to marriage certificate, 1948 p. 85

Amendment made on 28 January 1948.

Figure 34: The Westralia p. 86

HMAS Westralia, Virtual War Memorial Australia, https://vwma.org.au/explore/units/1342 accessed 5 May 2024.

Figure 35: Passenger Arrival card for Siegfried Hottelmann p. 90

Siegfried Hottelmann, Incoming passenger cards, National Archives of Australia, series A1197, item 9788232, p. 589.

Figure 36: Map of Europe p. 92

National Geographic Magazine, Washington, Dec 1983.

Figure 37: Family tree with Glenn Martin and Ellen Royall p. 95

Diagram by the author.

Figure 38: Carrs Park in the 1920s p. 96

Photograph, view to the south-west along the beach adjoining Carss Point during the mid-1920s, following the opening of the park to the public; Landscape Heritage Study for Carrs Bush Park, Kogarah Council, 2004, p. 24. (Fig. 27; source: Kogarah Historical Society.)

Figure 39. Plaque of Siegfried made in Tatura internment camp p. 98

Plaque of Siegfried Hottelmann at Tatura and District Historical Society Museum, donated by Sieglinde Hottelmann.

Bibliography

General References

Aliens Deportation Act 1946 (Cth), s. 3.

Ancestry.com, Bremen Passenger Lists, 1907-1939.

Australian Museums and Galleries, https://aumuseums.com/sa/

Australian War Memorial, Collection C327726.

Australians 1888, edited G. Davison, J.W. McCarty and A. McLeary, Fairfax, Syme & Weldon Associates, Broadway New South Wales, 1987.

Caledonian Maritime Research Trust, see Scottish Built Ships.

Carn Brae Port Pirie, https://carnbraeportpirie.com.au/

Gaden, Caroline, *From Baron to Battler*, 2012, ebook, https://www.smashwords.com/books/view/129058

Government Gazette Notices, Commonwealth of Australia.

Historical Boys Uniforms, German Boy Scouts (Pfadfinderen), https://histclo.com/

History of Hahndorf, https://hahndorfsa.org.au/history/

International Fund for Animal Welfare, https://www.ifaw.org/au

Knee, Lurline & Arthur, *Marched In*, published by Lurline & Arthur Knee for the Tatura & District Historical Society, 2008.

Laxon, W.A., *Huddart Parker: A Famous Australasian Shipping Company, 1876-1961*, Nautical Association of Australia, Melbourne, 2008.

Meerovskii, B.V., 'Johann August Von Einsiedel', The Great Soviet Encyclopedia, The Free Dictionary, 1979, https://encyclopedia2.thefreedictionary.com/Johann+August+Von+Einsiedel

Meiss, Corinna, Gluckauf: Emigration Desirable, *Traces*, 21st edition, 2022, pp. 14-16.

Monteath, Peter, *Captured Lives: Australia's wartime internment camps*, NLA Publishing, Canberra, 2018.

Morris, Jan, *Fifty Years of Europe: an album*, Villard, New York, 1997.

National Archives of Australia, Applications for Registration (Aliens Registration files), SP11/2.

National Archives of Australia, Internee Service and Casualty Forms, MP1103/2, PWN1355.

National Archives of Australia, Internee/Prisoner of War Service and Casualty Forms, MP1103/1, NF1649.

National Archives of Australia, Internee/Prisoner of War Service and Casualty Forms, MP1103/1, NF1650.

National Archives of Australia, Investigation Branch/Commonwealth Investigation Service - Correspondence Registers for Internees Inquiry, file series A367, C67918.

National Archives of Australia, National Security (Aliens Control) Regulations – Application For Leave To Submit Objections Against Detention Order, MP529/8.

National Archives of Australia, Passenger Arrivals Records, A1197.

National Archives of Australia, South Australia Police Gazette, D596, 1938/5650.

National Archives of Australia, Tatura Internment Camp, Victoria - National Security (Aliens Control) Regulations, MP529/8.

National Archives, Washington, US Arriving Passenger and Crew Lists.

Nayeri, Dina, *Who Gets Believed?*, Harvill Seeker, London, 2023.

New South Wales Government Gazette, Appointments, for Commission of the Peace.

New South Wales Registry of Births, Deaths and Marriages.

New South Wales State Archives & Records.

Nobility Titles, https://nobilitytitles.net/german-nobility-ranks/

Scottish Built Ships, https://www.clydeships.co.uk/

Smith, Eugene W., Trans-Atlantic Passenger Ships Past and Present, George H. Dean Co., Boston MA, 1947.

St Leon, Mark, 'The circus in the context of Australia's regional, social and cultural history', *Journal of the Royal Australian Historical Society*, Vol. 72, Pt. 3, Dec 1986, pp. 204-25.

U-boat.net, https://uboat.net/

Uncommon Lives: Klaphake, Wolf, http://uncommonlives.naa.gov.au/timeline.asp?lID=1

War Sailors, https://warsailors.com

Wikipedia, 'Crossing the inner German border during the Cold War'.

Wikipedia, 'Der Stahlhelm, Bund der Frontsoldaten'.

Wikipedia, 'Einsiedeln Abbey'.

Wikipedia, 'Forty Thousand Horsemen'.

Wikipedia, 'S.A.: Sturmabteilung'.

Wikipedia, 'Sydney Trocadero'.

Wikipedia, 'Wandervogel'.

Newspapers

Advocate (Burnie, Tasmania).

Auckland Star (New Zealand).

Barrier Miner (Broken Hill).

Border Watch (Mount Gambier, South Australia).

Cairns Post (Queensland).

Chronicle (Adelaide).

Coffs Harbour Advocate.

Courier-Mail (Queensland).

Daily Commercial News and Shipping List (Sydney).

Daily News (Perth).

Daily News (Sydney).

Daily Standard (Brisbane).

Daily Telegraph (Sydney).

Horowhenua Chronicle (New Zealand).

Hull Daily Mail (Hull, England).

New Zealand Herald (New Zealand).

Newcastle Sun (NSW).

News (Adelaide).

Oshkosh Daily Northwestern (Wisconsin, USA).

Otago Daily Times (New Zealand).

Poverty Bay Herald (New Zealand).

Recorder (Adelaide).

Smith's Weekly (Sydney).

Sydney Morning Herald.

The Advertiser (Adelaide).

The Age (Melbourne).

The Argus (Melbourne).

The Brisbane Courier.

The Herald (Melbourne).

The Register (Adelaide).

The Sun (Sydney).

The West Australian (Perth).

Uralla Times (NSW).

Waimate Daily Advertiser (New Zealand).

Western Daily Press (Yeovil, England).

Wingham Chronicle and Manning River Observer (NSW).

INDEX

Names of ships and titles of publications are given in italics.

Adelaide, 9, 14, 19, 27, 60, 71, 72, 78, 93
Adellen (ship), 10, 79
Aeon (steamer), 19–21
Alice Springs, 68, 70
Allied Works Councils, 53
America, 3, 10–11, 12–14, 31, 36, 69, 79, 94
Amsterdam, 10
ancestors of the family, 1
Antwerp (Belgium), 9
Application to object to detention order, 11, 13, 14, 48, 68, 73
The Argus (Melbourne), 4
Arncliffe, 22, 24, 29, 30, 32, 36, 39, 48, 50, 96
Auckland, 6
Australia
    German emigration, 93–95
    Jewish refugee arrival in, 15–16
    Laws on landing of aliens (non-British citizens), 4, 6, 34, 39
    Permanent residency in Australia granted for Siegfried, 20, 39
    post-war years, 81–82
    refugee views on, 14–16, 90

    Siegfried as a seaman on board Australian ships, 37

Bismarck, von Otto, 2
Boston, Massachusetts, 11
Boy Scouts, 71
Brazil, 13, 34
Bremen (Germany), 3, 91
Brisbane, 5
Britain, 10, 45, 63, 71, 87. *See also* England; United Kingdom
British Empire, 32, 37, 42
British government, 44
British Navy, 86–87
Buckley, Gertrude, 24, 32, 36
Bund of German Girls, 56
Burrell, H (British Products company)
    statements to the police on Siegfried, 30, 40

Canberra (merchant ship), 82
"Carn Brae" Port Pirie, South Australia, 19
Chemnitz (Germany), 1
Civil Aliens Corps, 53, 65
Cold War, 90
Collector of Customs, Port Adelaide, 20
Collector of Customs for South Australia, (Terry, F), 17, 20
Commonwealth Investigation Service, 32, 87–88
Count Heinrich von Einsiedel, 1–2, 11–13

Department of the Interior, Canberra, 20, 39
Deputy Director of Security, Melbourne, 54
Der Stahlhelm: Steel Helmet Organisation in Germany, 33, 73-74
Director-General of Security, Canberra (William Simpson), 53-54, 65
dredge, 17-18, 71
Dresden (ship), 2-3, 15, 72

Einsiedel Dam (Saxony), 1
Einsiedel family pledge, 13, 82
Einsiedel, von, family, 1, 79
England, 10, 35, 66, 90
Europe, 1, 8, 9, 44, 65, 66, 81

"Forty Thousand Horsemen", 27-28
Free German National Committee in Moscow, 1
Fremantle, 17
Frerck, Johannes
    deported to Germany, 58
    family, 55
    at internment inquiry 1946, 57-58
    leader of the Sydney Nazis, 57

Geneva Convention, 61
German Consul/Consulate, 68, 75, 76-77
Germany

division: West and East after World War II, 89-91
German ships in trade and transportation, 15
immigration of Germans to Australia, 6, 93-94
National Day, commemoration, Sydney, 57
opinions on position of Germany after the war, 62-63
post-internment: repatriation to Germany, 55-57
youth organisations in, 71-72
Great Britain. *See* Britain
Gustav (ship), 3-4, 71, 73, 93

Hagen (ship), 11
Hahndorf, South Australia oldest German settlement in Australia, 94
Hamburg, 11, 72, 79, 91
Hanover, 39, 78
Harz (Germany), 93
Hitler, Adolf, 1, 30, 33, 37, 43, 50, 57, 72, 74, 76, 89. *See also* Nazi party, Nazis
Hitler Youth Movement, 56, 72
Holzminden, 2, 90-91
Hottelmann, Siegfried
    birth, 2
    aristocratic heritage, 1-2, 15, 25, 39-40, 50, 66
    Einsiedel, von, Ilse (baroness) (mother), 1-2, 12, 66

Hottelmann, Maximilian
(father), 2, 39, 66
Einsiedel, von (grandfather),
68, 72
characteristics, 2, 4, 50–51,
72
arrival in Australia, 1, 4, 11
Australia, views on, 14–16, 90
marriage, 4, 23, 24, 29
children, 13, 22, 34, 39, 59,
81, 90
Count Heinrich von Einsiedel:
relationship, 11–13
education for the role of
Baron, 2
Rostock University,
Economics degree, 11
permanent residency in
Australia, 20, 24, 39
return to Germany, 10, 78
overseas travels, 10–11, 13,
89–90
passports, 11, 20–21
in America, 10–11, 14, 79, 94
relatives, 13
jobs on farms in Victoria, 4
as seaman, 2–4, 8–9–10, 11,
14, 15, 19, 26–30. *See also*
Dresden, Adellen, Aeon,
Gustav, Magdeburg,
Ormuz, Zeppelin
desertion of the ship
"Tisnaren", 15–17
as salesman in British
Products, complaints by
Burrell, 30
as a winchman at Port Pirie,
17

"Forty Thousand Horsemen":
role of German officer,
27–28, 68
Wirth's Circus, as elephant
driver, 5, 54, 68, 82
police reports and suspicions,
29–33, 35–41
"Alien Resident in Australia"
registration, 29
member of the Steel Helmet
Organisation (Der
Stahlhelm) in Germany:
33, 73-74
internment, 42
Hottelmann, Siegfried:
internment
in internment camp
associates in the camp, 55–58
desire to stay in Australia, 59
health issues, 52–53, 68
concept of internment as a
family, 48–49
interview with Justice
Simpson, 66–69, 71
joined by wife and child, 50–
51
refusal of release, 68
revoking the detention
orders, 80
Tatura camp, Victoria, 42–45
life after the internment
birth of a son, 81
in the crew of *Westralia*, 86–
88
as Justice of Peace, 90
moved to Rockdale, 81, 86
naturalisation, 89–90
residing at Revesby, 81, 86

as a sailor on merchant ship, Canberra, 82
death, 92
Howard Smith, 21, 26, 29–30, 32, 68

Immigration and Passports Officer, Melbourne, (Penhallhuriack,FJR), 18
internment camps: World War Two, 42–47
Internment inquiry 1946; Justice William Simpson, 2, 4, 5, 8, 10–11, 15–16, 25–26, 30, 48, 58, 80–81
Invercargill (New Zealand), 6
Ireland, 3–4, 93
Israel, 61

Jewish people, 16, 20, 44, 45, 58, 61

Katoa (steamer), 7
Klaphake, Wolf, 77

Laws on landing of aliens (non-British citizens), 4, 6, 34, 39
London, 10, 20, 35, 73, 94
Long Bay Penitentiary, 42

Macedon (steamer), 26, 29, 32
Macksville(New South Wales), 8
Magdeburg (ship), 8–9, 78
Melbourne, 3–4, 5–6, 7, 14, 19, 26, 30, 32, 71

Middle East, 87, 89
Milora (steamer), 5
Minister for interior, 17
Moore, Beatrice "Trix," 52–53
Mungana (steamer), 17, 21

National Socialism, 75
Nazi Party, 33, 57, 60, 74–78
Nazis, 34, 37, 41, 45, 51, 54–55, 57, 75
Newcastle, 26, 30, 31, 32
New Guinea, 45, 49
New South Wales, 8, 43, 55, 57, 70, 93, 100
New York, 3
New Zealand, 5–6, 22, 54, 68

Objection to detention order. See Application to object to detention order
Ormuz (ship), 3

Palestine, 28, 45, 61
Picker, Fritz, 56, 58
Port Adelaide., 20, 67, 94
Port Kembla, 19, 26
Port Pirie, 17, 19, 26, 27
prisoners of war, 42, 44, 46, 53, 61

Queensland, 15, 43, 70, 93, 94
Queenstown (Ireland), 3, 4

Recorder (Adelaide), 16
refugee migrants: rules for entry to Australia, 20.
refugees, 15–16, 20, 66

Reichstreue, 51, 76, 78, 79
Revesby, 81
Rockdale, 81, 84
Rookwood Cemetery, 92
Royall, Blanche (mother), 25,
    69
Royall, Ellen
(wife of Hottelmann,
    Siegfried)
  children, 39, 59, 81
  in boarding house at
    Arncliffe, 24
  first meeting with Siegfried
    at Trocadero, 22
  internment and joined with
    Siegfried, 48, 50, 68
  internment inquiry 1946:
    evidence, 49, 65
  internment inquiry1946:
    interview with Justice
    William Simpson, 69-70
  marriage, 25-26
  registered as "alien resident
    in Australia", 35
  relative of Glenn Martin's
    father, 4
  sisters, 50, 61, 64, 70
  death, 92
Royall, Herbert (father), 25-26,
    69
Russia, 1, 11, 63, 82

S.A. Sturmabteilung, (storm
    troopers), 75-76
Samuelson, Knut Berner, 16-17
San Francisco, 14
Saxony, 1, 78, 82, 83, 86, 89-
    90, 93

Sea Scouts, 67, 71-72
Simpson, William (Justice), 2,
    15, 26, 30, 49, 53-54, 58,
    65-67, 69-71, 75, 76, 80,
    84, 88
South Australia, 17, 20, 39, 43,
    45, 49, 93-94
South Australian Police Gazette
    21 September 1938, 17
Stassfurt (ship), 15
Sub-Collector of Customs, Port
    Pirie, 20
Sydney, 6, 7, 9, 19, 21-22, 26,
    27, 29-30, 33, 42

Tatura internment camp,
    Victoria, 42-47
Tisnaren (ship), 14-15, 21, 35,
    68, 75, 83-84
Toc H, Melbourne, 73
Trocadero, 22-23

Ulimaroa (ship), 8
United Kingdom, 4, 86
  declaration of war against
    Germany, 4, 57
USSR: Union of Soviet Socialist
    Republics, 89-90. See
    also Russia

Victoria, 4, 5, 42, 70, 71, 73
Vifstarval (Sweden), 3

Waranga Hospital, 52, 54, 59,
    68
Wellington (New Zealand), 6, 8
Westralia (ship), 89

William McArthur (ship), 30
Wirth's Circus, 5–8, 22
World War I, 2, 3, 15, 28
World War II
  outbreak, 1, 2, 4, 10, 27–40,
      42
  internment camps in
      Australia, Tatura,
      Rushworth, and
      Murchison, 42–47
  effects
      destruction of Europe,
      81–82
      division of Germany, 90–
      91
      post war issues in
      Australia, 81-82

Zeppelin (ship), 3

www.ingramcontent.com/pod-product-compliance
Lightning Source LLC
Chambersburg PA
CBHW052111090426
42741CB00009B/1763